NAPA

THE TRANSFORMATION
OF AN AMERICAN TOWN

50th Anniversary Celebration of Sawyer Tannery in 1919.

DEDICATION
TO MY GRANDPARENTS DAVE AND BETTY,
WHO TAUGHT ME TO BE A HISTORIAN OF HOME.

NAPA

THE TRANSFORMATION
OF AN AMERICAN TOWN

LAUREN COODLEY

ARCADIA

Published by Arcadia Publishing,
an imprint of Tempus Publishing, Inc.
Charleston SC, Chicago, Portsmouth NH, San Francisco

Printed in Great Britain.

Library of Congress Catalog Card Number: 2003114580

For all general information contact Arcadia Publishing at:
Telephone 843-853-2070
Fax 843-853-0044
E-Mail sales@arcadiapublishing.com
For customer service and orders:
Toll-Free 1-888-313-2665

Visit us on the Internet at http://www.arcadiapublishing.com

Front cover: Cecil Mathews (in the dark shirt) and his brother Joseph (far left) pose with their motorcycle club in 1922.

CONTENTS

ACKNOWLEDGMENTS

The work of many historians was helpful to me in thinking about how to write the history of my town. Thanks to Linda Heindenreich for her brilliant revisionist history and to Lin Weber for her excellent use of primary sources, both of which informed this book. I also wish to thank Dorothy Bryant for her original research into the history of the state hospital, Rebecca Yerger for her fine work in tracing the personal stories of longtime Napans, and to Jane Smith for sharing her beautiful and poignant essays. James Loewen, Michael Parenti, and Joseph Amato have helped shape my historiographical approach.

In my 30 years as a community college teacher in Napa, I have been educated and inspired by many of my students. Their efforts are reflected in some of the essays and oral histories in this book. Librarian Stephanie Grohs was an indispensable aide in my research. For assistance with editing, I want to thank Danielle Alexander and Dr. Steve Watrous.

This book is a reflection of the generosity of the people of Napa, who shared their memories, stories, and photographs with me. I want to especially thank Sudie Pollock, Rachel and Larry Friedman, Olamae Combellack, Dana Banks, Dennis Patterson, Bob Northrop, and Julian Weidler for allowing me to review and draw from their collections, memorabilia, and archives. For sharing or scanning images, thanks to Mike Mostafanejad, Chris Carlson, and Dan Graham. I greatly appreciate all those who agreed to be interviewed, many of whom appear in these pages. Thanks to the California State Library and the Napa County Historical Society for the many images from their carefully preserved collections, and to Al Edminster of the Napa Firefighters Museum for his efforts to keep the true history of Napa alive.

I am grateful to Arcadia Publishing and my editor Rob Kangas for their faith in my version of history. To my assistant Alison Tuthill, and my friend Cathy Mathews, my deepest thanks for your contributions and your astute observations as third and fifth generation Napans. My children, Caitlin and Nils McCune, have been enthusiastic and thoughtful readers throughout this process. Thanks to all of you who helped me present a different history of Napa, one that should not go unrecorded.

INTRODUCTION

Every new generation must rewrite history in its own way; every new historian, not content with giving new answers to old questions, must revise the questions themselves—since historical thought is a river into which none can step twice.

—R.G. Collingwood

In the late nineteenth century, the land where indigenous people had camped by the river and gathered acorns under the oaks for 10,000 years was transformed. European settlers developed cattle ranches and wheat fields, which later became fruit orchards and dairies. These farm lands surrounded Napa into much of the twentieth century, even as factories were established along the banks of its river. Throughout the twentieth century, Napa remained a rural small-town, relatively inaccessible and largely ignored by outsiders.

As this book was written, the city of Napa was in the midst of a profound transformation, in which much of its visible history was fast disappearing. It had been "discovered" and the town that had once been little more than a pass-through point on the route to the wineries of the valley became a premier tourist destination. In a very brief time, Napa lost its notoriety as home to the mental hospital, and became inseparable from an image of luxury and easy-living. Housing prices shot up as the downtown was "revitalized" and vestiges of blue-collar life were removed.

While the town changed, many longtime Napans remain, and for them the past is a living, breathing shadow . . . for every "Pear Tree" development that goes up, they remember the row of pear trees that was there before. As busy intersections replace open fields, they remember childhood games in the grass. As their children leave town in search of affordable homes, they remember a time when few people left town and fewer newcomers came.

Although Napa is unique in some important ways, it has participated in many of the struggles that define American life. In the nineteenth century, Napans planted orchards and established industries so that men and women could earn a living away from the farms. In the twentieth century, Napa was a blue-collar community, in which men and women found good union jobs at local factories or at the nearby naval base.

INTRODUCTION

Young people participated in the anti-war movement and feminist activism, as their parents attended meetings at the Elks Lodge and the Womens Club.

This historical record is still largely hidden in yearbooks, family photo albums, and boxes of yellowing newsletters. It is this story that the new field of social history tries to tell. The stories I sought were not those of the rich and the famous, but of those heroic individuals who tried to save farmlands, raise wages, and create and maintain family businesses. I wanted to capture what ordinary Napans experienced throughout the last century, what they did for entertainment, and how they felt about this town. I wanted to record the memories of the past as I watched the town transform into something new.

And yet not all has changed, and the Napa of old continues on along the streets where tourists rarely walk. It is there in the old-fashioned family businesses still trying to survive. It is there in gatherings in backyards bursting with the fruit trees that still love the climate here. In this Napa, people drink beer and play softball, they bowl and buy tamales, they wait in line at Buttercream Bakery, and they remember and try to pass on to their children, and to inquiring historians, what life was like here in the almost vanished past.

Chapter One

THE WATER-GOING-OUT-PLACE PEOPLE

If they had a town here, it was made of what the woods and fields are made of, and is gone. One may listen, but all the words of their language are gone, gone utterly. They worked obsidian, and that stays; down there at the edge of the rich man's airport there was a workshop, and you can pick up plenty of chipped pieces, though no one has found a finished point for years. There is no other trace of them. They owned their valley very lightly, with easy hands. They walked softly here.

—Always Coming Home, Ursula Le Guin

The indigenous people of California lived with delicacy and wisdom as they developed intricate knowledge of the plants and animals they considered kin. Nowhere was this more true than in the area now known as Napa. Between five and two million years ago, eruptions from volcanic zones near Mt. St. Helena created a bowl-shaped depression with fine grain clays and sand deposited by the river. For over 20,000 years the valley floor was covered with oak woodland, providing homes for many birds and small animals and mammals such as steelhead salmon, freshwater eel, trout, deer, antelope, tule elk (herds of a hundred or more), black and grizzly bear, otter, mountain lion, quail, duck, the peregrine falcon, the California condor, the yellow billed cuckoo, and the California clapper rail.

The valley floor was also home to many vernal pools, small seasonal wetlands formed when winter rains fill a depression in impermeable ground. The pools allowed fairy shrimp and other freshwater crustaceans to hatch, salamanders and spade foot toads to mate, and migrant waterfowl and shorebirds to feed. Vegetation was thicker beside the river, which flooded regularly. Native grasses turned a grayish-green in the summer while the hills and mountains were covered with redwood, Ponderosa pine, and Douglas fir.

When the Spanish arrived, they called the people they found *Guapo*, meaning brave. English speaking settlers changed the name to Wappo. The "Wappo" were actually three separate groups who spoke similar languages and lived in the foothills and valleys of what is now called the Mayacama Mountains. The Mishewal inhabited Alexander Valley and Lake County, and the Mutistul lived in eastern Sonoma County. The third group, the Mey'ahkmah, resided in the southern tidal areas of Napa, known as The Water Going Out Place. Anthropologists believe that people came here in waves, beginning more than 10,000 years ago. Their language was distinct from their Pomo neighbors and was similar to the Yuki of Mendocino, from whom they were separated 500 to 1,000 years earlier. Other language groups, such as the Patwin and the Suisun, lived around them in Vallejo and Fairfield.

The Mey'ankmah lived in small villages, which were near water, but above flood plains. Small campsites were at springs, on game trails, or near acorns. The huts, which were domed, were clustered around a sweathouse, and the largest such gathering would be about 40 huts. The huts were made of posts in a circle and the spaces between them were filled with sticks and tules. Each family had its own fire pit and smoke hole. Areas of the floor were filled with pillows of dry grass and ferns.

Acorns were their primary plant food, and there was also abundant shellfish, salmon, and deer. The entire tribe traveled together once a year to the Sonoma Coast, where they gathered abalone, clams, crabs, mussels, dry seaweed, and salt. They also walked to Clear Lake in the spring and summer, where they caught and dried fish and carried them home. Their paths were the origins of today's Highway 29, as well as Silverado Trail and Monticello Road.

The Mey'ankmah harvested clamshells from Bodega Bay and then worked them into flat round beads and drilled their centers. The value of the beads increased with their scarcity, so they were sold mainly to inland people. Discs could be used to buy bone-awls, baskets, dice, or arrows, or traded for tule mats from the Pomo in Lake County and for sinew-backed bows with peoples from Colusa. They also traded obsidian, which they made into shafts, spears, and arrowheads. Obsidian was formed from the Pliocene eruptions at Glass Mountain in the northern part of the valley.

The male chief ruled by consent and although individuals owned their own tools or jewelry, land was owned in common. The chief helped with preparing food, weaving blankets, and making fishnets. Men went to sweathouses twice daily to purify themselves, smoke, and tell stories. The sweathouses had dirt roofs, with one door facing south. Each one had a round pit and a flat cottonwood plant used as a foot drum. Sweathouses were built by both men and women. Puberty rites were reserved for girls only; women were separated from the tribe during menstruation and childbirth. Each month while their wives menstruated, men were not allowed to hunt, fish, gamble, dance, or eat meat or fat. Instead, they gathered acorns, rested, and smoked.

Although usually women gathered food and men hunted, tasks were occasionally traded. Women caught rabbits and pigeons in wicker traps. Men hunted deer as a group; one man wore a deer's head and lulled the animal into target distance. From deer they obtained meat and marrow, skins for clothing, and brains for cleaning and curing hides. From their bones they made needles and awls; in antlers they molded chipping tools for obsidian; from sinew bow strings were created; hooves were the source for dance rattles; from knuckle bones they made game pieces for gambling; and children created tops of acorns and dolls of sticks, stones, pebbles, and clay pellets. Games, dancing, and music were a constant part of native life; dance leaders were also tribal doctors. Adults played musical instruments such as bone flutes, elderberry wood whistles, and deer hoof rattles.

For the Mey'ankmah the plant world was sacred and central. They used many methods of resource management, including pruning, weeding, and aeration through tilling. They took only as many plants as they needed, and when they gathered seeds for pinole they would cast a few handfuls back to the ground to assure a yield the following season. When they gathered bulbs and tubers, they aerated the soil with digging sticks, creating a medium to yield large bulbs the next year. This constant aeration of the soil encouraged root growth for plant vigor and stimulated the kind of plants necessary for basket making. They would also coppice their shrubs, almost cutting them to the ground, which encouraged plants to flourish and stimulated re-growth of the long, straight, slender branches needed for tool and basket making. The people did not cultivate the earth, but they did periodically burn the landscape to control underbrush and stimulate acorn and bulb growth.

Each plant had multiple uses. The ghost pine, which the Mey'ankmah called *Nayo*, had nuts that were cracked and eaten raw or roasted. The roots were dug up with a stick and used for weaving large twine baskets. The cones provided fuel for fires and the pitch was chewed like gum. Hazelnut, called *Miti sohol*, had nuts which were dried in their shells and eaten later as desired. They were sometimes roasted prior to consumption. The shoots were used to make baskets for babies and for animal traps, and the wood was used for digging sticks. Madrone, called *Napayoko*, offered berries that were eaten fresh or tossed in a basket of hot coals, and the cooked fruit was stored for the winter. Healing infusions (medicines) were made from the bark and leaves.

Black Oak, called *Khothis*, was central to the lives of the people. Its acorns were gathered in large quantities and stored in specially built caches. Men and women gathered these acorns and worked together to harvest. Women alone had to dry, shell, grind, and leech the nuts before they could be cooked. Shelled acorns were pounded in a stone mortar made of igneous rock (such as basalt), stored beside a creek to remove the bitter tannin, and made into mush, soup, and bread.

Willow shoots, called *Chupe Pote*, furnished tea to treat diarrhea and were used for baby and acorn baskets, fish traps, and the foundation of coiled baskets. Shoots were the framework for the shelters, and bark was used much like aspirin. The toyon, called

Unu Ciwa Hoe, offered berries that were eaten after being baked or roasted in a basket of hot coals. The angelica flower, called *Ciwhel*, was eaten raw and root scrapings were rubbed on painful areas of the body. The fumes of the root were inhaled to treat colds, while root tea was used to reduce fevers. Sections of root were worn to protect against misfortune while ground up roots were rubbed on the arms for luck and scrapings of the root were smoked.

The California bay, called *Cuse*, offered nuts that were roasted in their shells, ground into flour, and formed into cakes. Leaves were boiled and used to treat rheumatism; branches of leaves were rubbed over the body as a germicidal and placed above doorways to keep sickness away. The manzanita, called *Mota Cano*, had berries that were eaten fresh or dried and ground into meal. Its leaves were ingredients in teas to treat diarrhea and stomach trouble. Its wood was used to make double-pointed fish hooks, harpoon heads, and bull-roarers (flat pieces of wood spun at the end of a long string).

Buckeye nuts were pounded, leached in a sand basin, and baked for several hours to be made into soup, mush, or gruel. Buckeyes were used only when acorns were scarce. Women used the stems and twigs of Redbud, called *Phopiel*, for water-tight baskets, which were peeled and split to create reddish-brown patterns. Feathers, clamshells, and beads adorned these baskets. Stalks of the Pacific Rush were used to string clam beads for their final shaping and polishing. Women made more decorative baskets, while men created baskets for gathering and fishing from unpeeled willow. These containers were given as gifts, cooked with, and used for storage.

Blue Elderberry, called *Kate*, had berries that were eaten fresh, cooked like acorn mush, or stored for winter. Tea was made from its flowers for children's fevers, while its branches were made into whistles, dance rattles, and staves used by women for their dice games. Even poison oak leaves were gathered and used in cooking to spice up dishes or as a dye for baskets. Fresh leaves were used on rattlesnake bites, and children were fed bits of poison oak leaves to immunize them.

The Mey'ankmah devised additional ways to flavor their food. They mixed into their acorn dough a little red clay, as well as bay leaves, which protected the acorns from rodents. They would not eat skunks, snakes, lizards, or frogs; there was a taboo against eating coyote, an animal which was considered almost sacred. They did eat turtle meat and eggs. Families ate two meals a day—one in the morning and one at sundown.

The Mey'ankmah had poetic names for the lunar months, such as Clover moon, Acorn moon, or Moon of Falling Leaves. They recognized constellations and knew six directions: East, West, North, South, Up, and Down. Their primary colors were red, blue, yellow, and pink. Their numerical system was based on fives, using their fingers and toes.

The tribe practiced the Kuksu religion, which shared common cosmology and ritual with other indigenous peoples throughout central California. The Mey'ankmah believed that the original world, in which the Old Ones (gods) had dwelled in peace and harmony, had been destroyed by ice, fire, and flood. When the water subsided Coyote and his grandson, Chicken Hawk, found the dry tip of Mount St. Helena, and Coyote made the Mey'ankmah from feathers. Chicken Hawk and Coyote went to the moon for the gifts of speech, movement, laughter, and eating. Moon sent down acorn mush and pinole. Owls and hawks were considered powerful spirits and Kuksu sacred dances used feathered cloaks and headdresses of these birds.

A celebration was held once a year for four to seven days to bring good health and luck to the community. It took place in either a permanent dance house or one built specifically for the occasion. The ceremony closed with a visit from the dead; on the last day, a ghost came down from the hills into the dance house to sing, dance, jump in and out of the fire, and return to the hills.

The Mey'ankmah believed in cremation, since ghosts were believed to haunt gravesites. Bodies were burned on piles of dry wood facing the head to the south, the direction the spirit would take on its way to the abode for the dead. But by the 1860s, Catholic priests insisted that they substitute burial for cremation.

Ursula LeGuin is the daughter of anthropologists Alfred and Theodora Kroeber, who studied and lived with Ishi, the "last California Indian." LeGuin grew up in the Napa Valley and wrote about its indigenous people in her fable of the future:

> I can stand here in the old pasture where there's nothing but sun and rain, wild oats and thistles, no cattle grazing, only deer, stand here and shut my eyes and see: the dancing place, the stepped pyramid roofs, a moon of beaten copper on a high pole over the Obsidian. If I listen, can I hear voices with the inner ear?

Chapter Two

BY "CHOICE" AND BY FORCE

Traces of the changing world vanish daily—and local historians do not take measure of them. Like generations before us, we fail to grasp what the world makes of us.

—Tulard Thuillier, *Histoire Locale et Regionale.*

The name California was inspired by Garcia de Montalvo's sixteenth-century Spanish novel *Las Sergas de Esplandian.* Its hero visits California, an island full of powerful women, whose Queen, Califia, "excited the imagination of many a Spanish soldier who read it," according to Andrew Rolle. Cortez wrote to the Spanish king about this novel after his conquest of Mexico in 1520, and the Spaniards began their exploration and colonization of the land we now know as California with the entrance of Juan Cabrillo's ships into San Diego in 1542.

The Spanish era in Alta California lasted from 1769 to 1821, when Mexico declared its independence. For the next 25 years, California was a Mexican state. During this time California was populated by the mission fathers, civil and military officials, and a handful of large landowners, most claiming Spanish descent, called *Californios.*

Napa (from the Patwin word for grizzly bear) was where the Mey'ankmah ran mission cattle and where *Californios* with Mexican land grants and landless Mexican soldiers met to organize campaigns against indigenous communities. After the Sonoma Mission was built in 1823, Napa and Sonoma shared a history because *Californio* men spent time in Sonoma while their wives stayed in Napa to manage the family ranchos.

Spanish colonialism was notable for the rigid racial hierarchy that determined one's rightful place in society. In Alta California, all people with a quarter or less Indian ancestry were eventually regarded as Español. The roots of racial thinking that the Spanish brought to the Americas were drawn from the struggle of Spanish Christians against the Moors in Spain from 711 to 1492. Although Pope Paul had ruled that Indians were human and had rights to freedom and property, many Spanish colonizers enslaved them.

There was a religious dynamic to the Indian wars as well. Spanish soldiers called on Saint James for divine assistance when they went into battle against indigenous people. Some colonizers referred to Indians as Moors and Jews. Pioneer Napa settler

George Yount wrote that General Mariano Vallejo "had bravery worthy of any Hidalgo who ever charged among the Moors in Spain."

When the Spanish established a mission in Monterey in 1770, indigenous people fled with stories of missionary life and the diseases that were spreading. Chronic depression due to captivity, unsanitary living conditions at the mission, and malnutrition all contributed to the sharply increasing death rate of indigenous peoples. In 1806, a measles epidemic swept through Mission San Francisco de Asis (Mission Dolores), killing 880 people and almost all of the children. Some survivors left the mission for Napa. Between 1809 and 1818, many of the Mey'ankmah from Napa were baptized at Mission Dolores and Mission San Jose. These new converts constructed the altars under the direction of the priests; those who resisted were lashed, pilloried, or chained in stocks.

Mission San Francisco de Solano (the Sonoma Mission) was founded two years after Mexico gained its independence. Father Jose Altimira, a cousin of Mariano Vallejo, wanted a mission north of San Francisco to discourage encroachment by the Russians or the Americans. The expedition, led by Altimira and Jose Sanchez, selected Sonoma as the site for the mission and presidio (a military fort designed to protect the mission padres against indigenous resistance and to make sure that the neophytes would not leave), and Napa as the place for mission cattle. Mexican soldiers prepared the region for settlement.

In its early years, the mission in Sonoma met with armed resistance from many of the Mey'ankmah, who came to the missions either by choice or by force. Some came out of necessity because the Spanish cattle grazing had destroyed community gathering grounds since the animals were put into the territory with the best seeds and roots. When their food was eaten by the cattle, some Mey'ankmah killed the cows to eat them. The Spanish, and later the *Californios*, arrested and punished such offenders. In addition, Vallejo and his brother Salvador often forced people into the missions. George Yount remembers capturing Mey'ankmah people and bringing them to the missions to be baptized.

Within the mission indigenous religion was replaced by Christianity, and the hunting and gathering society was replaced with agriculture. When native people entered the missions, priests insisted that they reinterpret their lives through Christian stories. Some tried to maintain their culture by incorporating indigenous spiritual symbols and practices into Catholicism. For the Mey'ankmah, Mass was a reminder of the new order. They were called to Mass by the same bells that called them to labor. As they filed into church, soldiers stood guard to make sure no one left the building before it was over. Many children were taken from their parents and raised by priests;

these children played musical instruments to accompany Mass and sat with the priests instead of their families. In Catechism, children were given gifts for reciting lessons correctly and were slowly turned away from their native religion.

Within the Sonoma Mission, priests allowed the Mey'ankmah people to do their dances for the amusement of visitors, sometimes gamble, take steam baths, and leave for several weeks, twice a year. The rest of their time was strictly controlled, and indigenous women had less means of resistance than men. While the priests allowed sweat houses, there were no menstrual rooms on mission grounds. Presidio soldiers as well as mission priests sexually exploited the women and disrupted their marriage customs, which involved fulfilling obligations to the mother-in-law and providing older women with status and security.

In the early 1830s, a group of trappers came from the Pacific Northwest to trade and unknowingly brought smallpox, and up to 75 percent of indigenous Californians died as a result. Salvador Vallejo estimated that 60,000 died in Sonoma alone. George Yount remembered, "After burning the bodies of their friends in heaps of hundreds, in despair the living fled to the mountains and wandered desolate and forlorn."

Overall, indigenous peoples developed a variety of survival strategies; some made treaties with the Spanish and Mexicans and learned their language, some joined missions, and some worked on the ranchos. Others fought against the soldiers, attacked the missions, and moved as far away from the colonizers as they could.

Two of the most powerful *Californio* families in the Napa area were the Vallejos and Juarezes. General Mariano Vallejo's father was Ignacio Vallejo, who held a certificate issued by the Inquisition certifying that he was of "pure" Spanish descent, "free of Indian, Negro, or Mulatto blood." In the late 1770s Ignacio Vallejo looked for a wife, considering only women of pure Spanish origin. When he found that Francisco Lugo and his wife were about to have a baby, he asked to marry their daughter. Fifteen years later, when he was 43 years old, he married the teenager.

Mariano Vallejo grew up at the Monterey Presidio. His family was educated and owned property. He began his military career at the age of 16 and proved himself by attacking tribal communities in a pre-emptive manner, while also making treaties with other indigenous people who would help him maintain Mexican rule. His most famous battle in Napa was in 1835. He persuaded Sam Yeto, a Suisun leader, to help him subdue the Mey'ankmah. Originally Yeto attempted to drive the *Californios* out, but was persuaded instead to work for General Vallejo. Vallejo gave him the name Chief Solano and the title "Chief of the unconverted Indians." After Yeto decided to join forces with Vallejo, a victory celebration was held and Vallejo gave him an honor guard dressed in full military uniform on horseback.

NAPA

Sam Yeto stole a woman to be his wife from the Chiuructos tribe while on an expedition with Vallejo in 1835. He brought her to the Sonoma mission where she was baptized, named Isadora, and taught by Father Lorenzo to be submissive to her husband. It was relatively common for soldiers and priests to allow men to take women from other tribes as trophies. In 1838 Yeto, Father Mercado, and a group of *Californios* and American immigrants kidnapped women and girls from a local community for sale to the soldiers at Fort Ross, and to men living on the other side of San Pablo and San Francisco Bays.

Most Mexican soldiers were *Mestizo*, the result of intermarriage between indigenous women and Spanish settlers. Wives and children followed the men to California, a tradition that had been part of Spanish and Mexican armies since the sixteenth century. Platon Vallejo describes in his memoir how a group of women camped out on the banks of the creek in what is now Santa Rosa, while their husbands fought indigenous people in Lake County. A soldier arrived to tell of the death of one of the men. When his wife heard, she seized her newborn infant and threw it into the stream and was about to throw herself when she was overtaken and stopped. A soldier rescued the baby and gave it to General Vallejo. Vallejo gave it to his wife, who had just suffered a stillbirth, to raise as her own.

The records of the Vallejo family furnish most of the information about the soldiers' lives. Salaries and uniforms seldom arrived on time; at the Sonoma Presidio, General Vallejo paid soldiers' salaries himself. Most landless Mexican immigrants remain nameless, much like the Mey'ankmah, who performed much of the hardest work on ranchos. The landless Mexicanos and the Mey'ankmah ran the *matanzas*, or cattle slaughters, for the land-holding families. The cattle was skinned and their fat (tallow) was melted into skin bags to be transported to trading ships. The carcasses were left for wild animals.

Californios benefited from the opening of international trade. A fur and tallow trade flourished, as well as commerce involving the coats of sea otters. Indigenous Aleuts, who were recruited by Russians from Alaska, were used to hunt the otters. *Californios* sold furs to New England maritime merchants as fur trappers hunted otters, seals, beavers, and mink to near extinction.

Mediterranean grasses were transported on the hooves of Spanish cattle and eventually these weeds and annuals replaced native grasses. Herds of domesticated animals consumed millions of acres of grasses and eroded hillsides and stream banks. Rodents, deer, antelope, and elk multiplied as they gorged on new European grasses. Grizzly bear populations grew as they began to hunt and eat domesticated animals.

Vallejo moved into the Sonoma Valley in 1835. He gave land grants to his favorite soldiers and friends; the first land grant he bestowed was not to a *Californio*, but to the

By "Choice" and By Force

American George Yount, who had come to Napa from Missouri in 1833. Yount won the favor of the priests by working as a carpenter in the missions, and he served in the Mexican army. He received a land grant north of Napa in the area now known as Yountville. Until the American invasion of 1846, Yount remained loyal to Vallejo, helping him battle native people whenever asked. Pioneer John Bidwell observed that Euro-Americans like Yount assimilated into the *Californio* culture and lived in every respect like the Spaniards.

Other grants in the Napa area included the Tulocay rancho to Cayetano Juarez, the Yajome rancho to Rodriguez, the Las Putas rancho to Berryessa, the Napa rancho to Salvador Vallejo, and the land by the Napa River to Nicholas Higuera. Any time the general needed help from these men to fight wars against the Mey'ankmah, he summoned them to meet at Los Trancas, his rancho, which was often the site of rodeos and bear fights.

Cayetano Juarez was a sergeant who helped Vallejo found the Sonoma Presidio. In 1837, when Mexico did not pay its soldiers, Sergeant Juarez organized a mass desertion to ride to Monterey and demand payment. Sam Yeto, working as a spy, reported the plan to Vallejo, who confronted the soldiers as they were mounting their horses, reminding them that capital punishment was the penalty for desertion. He frightened everyone but Juarez into staying, so Juarez left alone and swam across the Carquinez Straits with his horse. Just short of Monterey, he was captured and sentenced to be shot. Vallejo instead ordered Juarez to marry, and gave him a grant in Napa to help him "civilize" the region. In return, Juarez allowed Vallejo to direct his personal life.

Juarez built his first adobe on the Tulocay Rancho, which covered more than 8,800 acres. In 1845 and 1874, he built more houses to accommodate his growing family; big enough that once a year it held its own rodeo. His children attended school in Sonoma and spent their weekends in General Vallejo's home. At the Tulocay Rancho, over 400 indigenous people raised cattle and crops, but the rancho was not self-sufficient like the Vallejo hacienda. Cayetano's wife also performed manual labor and used local herbs for healing, cooking, and cleaning. Her children grew up speaking Spanish and Uluca, a Patwin dialect; one of her daughters spent long hours with the indigenous women at the rancho exchanging information regarding menstruation and childbirth. Domitila Juarez Metcalf, who grew up in Napa on the Tulocay Rancho, remembered a cholera epidemic in which Indian servants in the house "would die before their very eyes, and the men in the fields dropped in their tracks." According to her granddaughter Viviane Juarez Rose, Metcalf told her interviewer in 1920 that the Spanish did not contract the disease.

Men often left the ranchos and spent extended amounts of time socializing at the Sonoma Presidio. While they were away, their wives managed the estates. *Californianas* were trained in horseback riding and the use of small arms and they did not go out without their weapons due to fear of indigenous resistance. They were expected to produce large families: Maria Juarez had 11 children at Rancho Tulocay and Mariano Vallejo's wife had 16. The pressure on *Californianas* to reproduce was so strong that when one of the Juarez daughters entered the Dominican convent, her father was angry enough to threaten her with violence.

Because of the Mexican government's policy to secularize the missions, Vallejo dismantled most of the Sonoma Mission by the end of the 1830s. Indigenous people's lands were now used to graze cattle or were farmed by retired soldiers. Some native people worked for Vallejo at his Petaluma Hacienda. Their labor routine was similar to that of the missions: they were awakened at 5 a.m. for roll call and prayer, they breakfasted on atole, and they worked in the fields, candle factories, or leather shops until the end of the day. Others worked for George Yount or Cayetano Juarez in exchange for food. Six hundred worked on Salvador Vallejo's Rancho. When a rancho owner died, the entire work force often moved together to work for another owner.

The last great epidemic of the Mexican era took place in 1837. A group of men left Sonoma to get supplies from Fort Ross and came back with smallpox. In May 1838, Vallejo announced in a nation-wide communication that smallpox was raging on the northern frontier and was killing the Indians by the hundreds; later he said that 70,000 indigenous people died as a result. Juarez Vivian Metcalf writes: "The death toll was so great because the Indians used sweat boxes and then plunged into the water of the river," bringing on pneumonia. The troops of Sam Yeto (Chief Solano), Vallejo's assistant, were reduced from several thousand to 200 men who continued to ride into battle with Vallejo. Solano stayed to serve at Vallejo's side until the War with Mexico began in 1846.

The Mexican War was vigorously debated in Congress. It was opposed by Americans ranging from philosopher and writer Henry David Thoreau, who went to jail rather than pay taxes to fund it; to abolitionist Frederick Douglass, who wrote of "the present disgraceful, cruel, and iniquitous war with our sister republic." Irish workers demonstrated in New York and Massachusetts against the war, while others enlisted in the Mexican Army and formed the Saint Patrick's Battalion. Desertion by American troops from the war grew to a total of over 9,000 men. Nevertheless, Mexico surrendered in February 1848. Under the Treaty of Guadalupe Hidalgo, the United States was given possession of nearly half of Mexico, which included much of the Southwest as well as California.

By "Choice" and By Force

American settlers who came west brought with them a variety of racial attitudes, indicated by the curious origin of the term "greaser." Platon Vallejo wrote that English-speaking people called the hide and tallow merchants *Mantekueros*, or grease merchants, and considered it a compliment. It was only later that it became a slur against Mexicanos and *Californios*. On the other hand, Salvador Vallejo wrote that the people who came to Napa from Missouri were very dirty people. By the time they arrived over the Sierras, their hands, faces, and clothes were a greasy mess, so the *Californios* called them *Matecosas*, or greasers. The Missourians, after gaining power, began to call the indigenous people the same, and because Americans often failed to distinguish between Indians and *Californios*, the name was applied to both.

David Weber reminds us that "those of us who study history for a living understand very well that there are many truths." Just as a term like greaser can have a contested meaning, a war and its aftermath can be viewed with multiple perspectives. Indigenous people remember the transfer to American rule that occurred after the Mexican War as devastating. When George Yount had arrived in the mid 1830s, he described the Napa Valley as being inhabited by grizzly bears and Indians that were equally savage. Yount estimated that 8,000 Mey'ankmah lived in Napa, and he remembered when a band of armed men arrived on horseback with orders to "destroy and drive off into the mountains all the Indians of the Napa Valley." The men rode from rancho to rancho, killing men, women, and children. A group of *Californios* finally succeeded in stopping them and, after a brief skirmish, placed them under arrest. The men were never tried, due to the absence of an established justice system.

In 1847, Nathan Coombs and John Grigsby (who had participated in the short-lived Bear Flag Revolt in Sonoma) traded their carpentry skills to Nicholas Higuera, who paid for their services with land along the Napa River at the head of the tidewater. Nathan Coombs staked out a town site from the land that lies between Brown Street and the river and from Napa Creek to the foot of Main Street, a distance of about 600 yards. The town of Napa was to eventually evolve from a combination of several land grants: Higuera's grant became downtown west of the river, the land north of First Street had belonged to Salvador Vallejo, and the land east of the river was in the possession of Juarez and Rodriguez.

In 1849 another former Bear Flagger, James Marshall, was supervising a group of indigenous people working on mud flats on the American River. One of them showed him some gold flakes next to the sawmill they were building. Marshall told only John Sutter, hoping to keep it secret, but the secret did not keep. California became the center of a world migration by the end of that year.

Chapter Three

CIVILIZATION'S TRIUMPH?

In the birth, or rebirth, of pioneer culture, some groups were "losers," including Indians and Californios. They lost lives, lands, resources, livelihoods, autonomy, cultural dominance, and as in the case of many small native tribes, their very existence as peoples. Some, especially newly arriving settlers from the United States and Europe, and to an extent Latin America and Asia, including the few women pioneers, clearly "won." They secured new opportunities; their populations increased; they assumed political control; and their cultures took root and often flourished.

—Kevin Starr, *Rooted in Barbarous Soil*

Napa was a town that sprang up to meet the needs of gold miners. The first 20 years of Napa's history under American rule were as painful for native Californians as they were exciting for new settlers. Saloons were built, men were elected to serve in the new state of California, stage and train service was developed, and wheat became a major industry. Churches and schools opened, and gradually the memory of the indigenous and Mexican presence faded as new streets and buildings were named for American settlers.

After James Marshall discovered gold, tens of thousands of people came to California. Although most traveled from the East and Midwest of America, others came from Mexico, China, Chile, England, France, and Spain. Half of the Americans came from the eastern states by ship around Cape Horn or by steamship to Panama, crossing the Isthmus on foot. Americans from the Midwest took the Overland Route over the Sierra Nevada Mountains; as many as 10 percent of these over-landing forty-niners were female.

The American gold seekers were not poor, because the cost of getting to California was the equivalent of more than a year's worth of wages for the average American in 1849. Many of these travelers imagined that they would find a Utopian community where everyone would be rich and no one would have to compete. Instead, they found gold mining exhausting; most of them had never worked with their hands, and many failed to break even. They turned their hostility toward each other and the Mexican, Chinese, Chilean, and indigenous peoples. Kevin Starr comments that California during the Gold Rush "is not a pretty story; but it is a true story and it must be faced." Indigenous people were hunted by state-supported militia while Latino, Chinese, and African-American miners were driven from the most promising of the gold fields or otherwise suppressed, beaten, or outright murdered. Starr argues that this history must be integrated into the larger story of America's ongoing struggle with racial injustice.

Historian Brian Roberts notes that few Anglo forty-niners would have arrived in California as one-dimensional racists. Roberts suggests that since many American reformers had been writing about the plight of the vanishing Indian, the miners would have known about "the moral problems of Indian removal." Although many indigenous Californians were killed by miners, other Anglo observers recorded these atrocities "not," says Roberts, "because they were proud of these acts, but to criticize their fellows."

Unable to understand the native people, Americans called them "Digger Indians." An early Napa historian, C.A. Menefee, told his readers that:

> These people were a different race, lower in intelligence than any other upon the continent of America: It is simply impossible for any man to civilize a Digger Indian . . . at the first impulse, he returns to his vagabond life of idleness, his grasshopper diet and his wretched wigwam of bows. . . . [He believed that they] did not make the slightest advance in moral or religious culture in spite of the most zealous efforts of the Fathers . . . the whole subject of religion was beyond the reach of their untutored intellects.

In marked contrast, George Yount was impressed by the religious devotion of indigenous people. He saw travelers passing mounds that marked spirit places, carefully placing a bead, pin, seed, or a stone out of respect for the holding monument. He described the trance state as a communication with gods who were ghosts, and after returning from this state they would report what had been learned from the interaction. Richard Dillon says that Yount "saw their prophecies as Delphic; their frenzies as akin to the religious possession of the most religious Christians." Yount was illiterate, but he gave vivid interviews about the violence he witnessed by American settlers:

> They roamed from Rancho to Rancho, from Rancheria to Rancheria, and left behind only traces of tears and blood—they would shoot down the Indian and even the Spaniard for more sport, or as some have confessed

upon the gallows, "only to see them jump and struggle, and to hear them yell and groan."—They stole cattle by the hundreds from the Ranchos and drove them to market in the cities—they often entered houses on remote farms, and robbed in open daylight, prepared for murder indiscriminately if resisted, or in any danger of being exposed—sometimes they have been known, in organized bands, of from 20–50, to embark in an indiscriminate slaughter of all the Indians they could find. . . . On one occasion they even skinned their wretched victim alive from the sole of the foot to the crown of the head—and exultingly to mock and exult over his expiring agonies.

In 1850 California passed "An Act for the Government and Protection of Indians," making it legal for Americans to indenture indigenous children; boys could be kept until the age of 18 and girls until the age of 15. In 1860, the indenture laws changed to keep boys and men until the age of 25 and girls and women until the age of 21. Indigenous people were barred from testifying against white men in court. C.A. Menefee explained: "When young Indians were captured or kidnapped and made use of by white settlers for servants or slaves, they seldom lived for two or three years." He depicts them as "thronging the streets of Napa City in great numbers, occasionally fighting and always getting drunk. . . . They would, at times, make night hideous with their howling among the willows along the banks of the river, with what purposes or motives we are left to conjecture." Some were moved to reservations in Clear Lake, others to ranchos owned by Americans and *Californios*.

The *Napa Register* recorded on August 28, 1880 the obituary of Suzie Williams, "an Indian Girl, who was a faithful servitor." During this time, according to Yolanda Beard, some native women living in Napa County resorted to infanticide. The *Napa County Reporter* carried announcements of indigenous men found in the Napa River; although the newspaper only seems to mention indigenous people when they died or were arrested, census data shows that many were employed as laborers or servants. When a native man was found dead near the steamship landing, The *Napa Reporter* headlined it the "March of Civilization."

In the 1850s Napa was a mining town with few amenities, many hotels, and much liquor. As of 1852, it had only 300 permanent residents. Yet, as Kevin Starr has noted, "Something like an instinctive capacity for city making arrived in California with the Gold Rush. . . . Even the most solitary of miners required hardware and provisions from urban retail outlets, a cooked meal and a hot bath in a hotel or boarding house, and a glass of whiskey in a Main Street saloon."

NAPA

Harrison Pierce came to California to mine gold. In Napa he built the Empire Saloon, which fed gold miners beef, bread, and coffee during the winter, and lodged them for $1 a night. The lifestyle of these mining towns was one in which drinking, gambling, and fighting replaced family and church; a simple deck of cards was referred to as a "California prayer book." Nathan Coombs built the American Hotel in 1850 on Main and Third Street. Mariano Vallejo constructed a general store at the end of First Street between Napa Creek and Napa River. Although the city only had 40 wooden buildings, Norton King comments, "It was one of the busiest little towns in California . . . [with] a reading room, a well attended theater, a company of minstrels, a band of music, an agricultural society, and a jockey club."

At the California Constitutional Convention in Monterey, delegates had debated whether or not California should become a slave state. They decided to include in the constitution a prohibition of slavery, because the miners were insulted that slaves might do the same work as them. Although some advocated that all free blacks be banned from immigrating to California, the majority decided to create a constitution that opposed slavery, so they could join the Union. On November 30, 1849, the Constitution of California was put up for a vote and the white men of Napa, who voted at Pierce's Empire Saloon, endorsed it.

When California officially joined the United States in 1850, its flag was the Bear Flag. On February 8, 1850, Napa became one of California's original 27 counties; its boundaries extended to Lake County until 1861. John C. Fremont and William Gwin became the first U.S. senators, and Mariano Vallejo became a state senator. The city of Napa was named the county seat and plans were made to build its first courthouse. It was constructed on the east coast and shipped over by boat to the newly named Coombs Street in 1856. The County Jail was upstairs and the first recorded occupant was "Timothy Indian" in 1860.

Former gold miner William Thompson gave General Vallejo lumber to build what Vallejo hoped would be the state capital in the new town of Vallejo. However, the plan was abandoned due to bedbugs and the lack of amusement in Vallejo. In return for the lumber, Thompson received 320 acres of Vallejo's land and then bought more. American gold seekers were sick of the monotonous diet of beef and grain and were willing to pay high prices for fresh fruit. Thompson and his brother ordered saplings to be delivered by boat from the East Coast and planted the first peach and apple trees. They diverted and channeled Suscol Creek for irrigation, where they found the skulls of indigenous people who had died when Sam Yeto was still opposing Vallejo. By 1860 Thompson's Gardens were known all over the West, and 150,000 peach and apple trees had been planted.

Civilization's Triumph?

A depot at the Napa Hotel on First and Main Streets was the site of a stage line established by Smith Brown running between Sacramento, Sonoma, Petaluma, and Napa. Brown sold it in 1858 and bought land to grow wheat from Cayetano Juarez. While indigenous people had once harvested wheat at the missions using wild horses, now it was done with mechanical machinery pulled by domestic horses. After wheat was cut, it was piled in an open area and either baled for feed or winnowed, a process in which the grain was separated from the chaff. The grain was piled on horse-drawn wagons and taken to mills such as Stoddard or Bale. In 1873, C.A. Menefee commented, "There are fewer localities in the world where wheat will grow better than in the Napa Valley. . . . Oats and barley grow equally well with wheat . . . nearly the whole of the land in the valley is adapted to all kinds of cereals."

This era was a difficult one for the *Californios*. After 1850 the Rancho society was replaced by American towns and homesteads. The Land Act, proposed by Senator Gwin, was passed in 1851 by Congress. It established a board to evaluate *Californio* land claims. All rejected claims and unclaimed land were opened up to American settlers.

When the Senate debated the subject, Senator Thomas Hart Benton called it abominable because it would force *Californios* to sell their land to cover legal fees. He was correct in his assertion as Salvador Vallejo sold his cattle to pay lawyers to defend his ranch. He won the claim, but it was appealed and American settlers moved on the property. They burned his crops to drive him and his workers off the land. He held 3,000 acres until the Civil War, when he led *Californio* troops on the Union side, but while he was gone squatters took the rest of his land. By 1900 the Vallejo family owned nothing in the Napa Valley. The only *Californios* to retain land in Napa were the Juarez family. They donated 50 acres to the town as the Tulocay Cemetery in 1859, and the entire property in 1887 after Juarez's death.

By 1860 the majority of Mexicans in Napa, including *Californios*, lived in a neighborhood called Spanish Town. Most of the men in this neighborhood appear as laborers in the census, while women often ran boarding houses. Almost all *Californios* who had a land grant in the Napa Valley lost it to squatters, although John E. Brown claimed that he purchased Browns Valley for a "horse and a buggy." The Berryessa family held onto their land grant because they lived there, although they eventually had to sell it to squatters to pay their debts.

Ranching had become a risky investment in California. During the drought of 1864, historian Andrew Rolle says "the dust on the ranges was so dense that it clogged the nostrils of the dying animals." California's cattle herds deteriorated through inbreeding and although large ranchers imported meatier strains of beef cattle into California, small ranchers could not compete.

NAPA

Travelers had to swim their horses across the Napa River until ferries began to operate at Third Street in 1848. The first steamship, *The Dolphin*, began to run from Napa to San Francisco in 1850, carrying hay, lumber, coal, and passengers. Napa's streets were unpaved and composed of silt, which made it impossible for horses to walk across when it rained. Hay was dumped on pedestrian crossings in front of the hotels on First and Third Street, but it was not unusual for people to fall into mud up to their waists. The year's garbage would sink into the winter mud and disappear forever.

There was so much public drunkenness in 1855 that Napans almost voted for Prohibition, with a vote of 198 in favor and 205 opposed. In 1858 a telegraph line was laid between Napa and Vallejo, funded by 12 citizens who paid $100 each to put it down; for 50¢ a person could send a 10-word message over it. In 1862 a law was passed outlawing cattle, mules, horses, goats, or hogs to run loose in the city of Napa. In 1863, one writer commented irritably in the *Napa County Reporter*, "If a prize were to be awarded for the perfection of dullness, we should expect Napa City to be a prominent competitor." Yet that same year, when a laborer named Charles Brittan couldn't cash his paycheck, he took the steamer to San Francisco, bought a revolver, and shot his employer Joseph Osborne, owner of Oak Knoll Plantation. When Osborne died, Brittan's was the first official execution in Napa.

Local newspapers began publishing in the late 1850s. The *Napa County Reporter* was founded on July 4, 1856; by the 1860s, it represented the Democratic opposition to the presidency of Abraham Lincoln. A pro-Confederacy newspaper, the *Napa Echo*, was established and published in Napa until Lincoln's assassination. The *Echo*'s offices were in a brick building along Main Street. One of its advertisers, the Caucasian Shaving Saloon, was on the west side of Main Street near Second. The *Napa Register* was founded in 1863 to advocate for the Republican Party, as the city was deeply involved in the debates about the Civil War.

Napa historian Lin Weber writes, "There never was a rebel insurrection in Napa County, but there could have been." In 1863, 200 men developed an elaborate plan to cut the telegraph wires between Sacramento and San Francisco and take control of Napa. They intended to take a steamboat in the Napa River and launch an attack at Mare Island and the Benicia arsenal. From there they planned to capture additional ports until they could force the state to secede from the Union. Agents intercepted the would-be rebels in San Francisco.

Although the town was divided, as the war continued, a majority sided with the Union. Dr. Ben Shurtleff was a former gold miner and Union supporter who eventually became the first director of the Napa Insane Asylum. Nathan Coombs was one of the few Napans who actually joined the Union army in 1863, paying for his trip himself and returning to Napa in 1864 as a convention delegate for Abraham Lincoln's second term. When Lincoln was assassinated, a funeral was held in Napa with a funeral oration delivered by Henry Edgerton.

Many citizens were concerned about the lack of factories in Napa. Although limited manufacturing existed, such as the vineyard plows made by M.P. Rose of Carneros, the gang plows made by the Manual family of Napa City, and the planing mills owned by J.A. Jackson, C.A. Menefee commented wistfully in 1873, "Nothing but the capital and enterprise are lacking to make Napa an important manufacturing place." He pointed out, "Besides the facilities of the railroad for travel, all the conveniences for water privileges are afforded. Rents are low, fuel is cheap and abundant." F.A. Sawyer established the Sawyer Tanning Company in 1869 as a wool pullery. He had seen local butchers throwing away sheep skin and began to remove the wool for profit. His father joined him in 1870 and they built a facility to tan the sheepskins. Emmanuel Manassee, a German immigrant, moved to Napa with his wife in 1871 to work for Sawyer. By 1874 the Napa City Tannery had also been established, and both tanneries used the river to transport hides.

Sam Brannan was an entrepreneur who had visited the spas of Europe and decided to set up his own in 1862. He named it Calistoga and located it to the north of the city of Napa. Lin Weber describes it as a kind of "nineteenth-century theme park." Brannan wanted residents of San Francisco to patronize his spa, so he partnered with Nathan Coombs to open a stage coach line. Passengers would get off the steamboat at Suscol and be met by Coombs and Brannan's coaches drawn by six horses. They could either rest at the Suscol House Hotel, or go directly up to Calistoga.

Brannan also wanted a railroad to transport his visitors, and he persuaded the state legislature to propose a bond. The first engine, called the *Calistoga*, came into Napa in 1865. In 1866, the Napa Valley Railroad was laid down from Suscol to connect with the California Pacific Railroad at a place called Napa Junction. There were stops at Thompson Station, the Napa Depot at Suscol and Fourth Street, or the West Napa Depot on California Street. Service was extended to Calistoga by 1868. Forests were felled on the hillsides for the wood-burning furnaces on the trains; eucalyptus trees were imported from Australia with the mistaken idea that they could be used for fuel or railroad ties.

Historian Joseph Amato explains that many American towns were constructed according to the railroad's visions of what regional agricultural centers should be. Each Main Street was wide enough to allow a wagon to turn around and "The lumber yard sat adjacent to the tracks; the bank was always at First and Main, the first churches (Episcopal, Presbyterian, and Methodist) were built in the vicinity of Third

Street." And so it was, in Napa City, by 1870. Nathan Coombs donated land for the Methodist Church, built in 1858, and for the Presbyterian Church, built in 1874; both were in the vicinity of Third Street. Saint John's Catholic Church was constructed on Main Street in 1858.

Napa's first grammar school, the Central School, was built in 1868 on the site of what is now City Hall and children could attend up to the eighth grade. Napa Collegiate Institute, a co-ed school built in 1860, was eventually run by the Methodist Church. The Napa Ladies Seminary, built in 1869 on Seminary Street, offered Math, English, Latin, French, Italian, Science, Music, and Painting to its students. Sophie Alstrom, daughter of Swedish immigrants who had opened a spa in St. Helena in 1850, was able to attend the Napa Ladies Seminary after the railroad was built. She later taught art there and produced beautiful paintings of Napa wildflowers like Columbine and Fairy Lantern. Civilization had indeed triumphed, and Napa was poised for its future as a center of orchards, mills, and tanneries.

Chapter Four

CHINESE BANDS AND

ASYLUM ORCHARDS

The landscape that took shape reflected the goals of the people who settled there. Nothing about California's natural environment made specialized crops more available. Advantages exist only in the imagination: they are the riches that people read into soil, and climates and water.

—Steven Stoll, The Fruits of Natural Advantage

Between 1870 and 1900 Napa took shape as an American town, with the development of agriculture and industry to sustain the population and the building of a beautiful downtown center where people would meet and greet their friends for the next 100 years. Wheat farming gave way to fruit farming, a Chinese community settled into houses alongside Napa creek, an Asylum for the Insane opened its doors, and Napans joined the campaigns for temperance and suffrage that flourished at the end of the century.

The river furnished access to transportation as lumber yards, warehouses, and wharves were constructed along the waterfront. Steamers carried both industrial and agricultural products, and sometimes even entire flocks and herds of livestock. Sawyer Tannery and Stoddard Milling built factories next to the river in order to ship their goods to San Francisco and beyond. The California Glove Company opened in 1876 on Soscol Avenue, employing almost 300 people; the Napa Woolen Mill opened in 1885, producing blankets for the military; and Evan's Shoe Company opened in 1897. The train functioned as the other source of transportation, with a rail line that had been built between Napa and Calistoga in 1867, and which was acquired by Southern Pacific Railroad in 1875.

By 1889 California was the second largest producer of wheat in the nation, and Napa County was second only to Santa Clara County as a leading wheat producer in the state. It was Napa's primary crop, supplying over 10 percent of all grain in the country. The wheat boom required men to work in the fields for eight weeks a year and follow the harvest. These workers were commonly referred to as "bindle stiffs." Stories were told in Los Angeles in the 1850s about the "slave mart" in which indigenous people who had been part of the missions were "sold" for a week at a time, and bought up by the owners to work the harvest.

Critics of large scale wheat farming saw it as the same get-rich-quick thinking that had doomed the gold miners. Cletus Daniels argues that "family farming gave life to humane and enduring society, while large scale farming created only personal fortunes." By 1900 most small ranchers had lost their wheat farms to large growers, wheat growing had depleted the soil, and overproduction reduced prices. Steven Stoll writes, "With no more cheap land to bust, farmers abandoned their dismal acres, leaving behind a desolation that was the agricultural equivalent of ripped out gold hills."

California agriculturalists then turned to horticulture. Luther Burbank's experiments with garden crops in Santa Rosa promoted the production of fruits and vegetables. With the development of high-speed freight service to the East Coast, Napa's fruit production expanded, creating a major agricultural industry. The moderate climate, the availability of land (even for people with limited income), the increased demand for fruit within the state, and the glamour that out-of-state consumers attached to fruit products from California all combined to produce what historian Steven Stoll describes as "the center of fruit production in North America, with the rural landscape that looked like nothing the United States had never seen before."

The "French Prune" was introduced to California by a San Jose nurseryman from France, Louis Pellier. *Sunsweet* historian Robert Couchman comments, "The problem was to produce a dried prune of better quality that would have a chance to displace the imported product into the United States." Botanically speaking, a prune is a plum, but not all plums can become prunes. A fresh plum variety, known as the prune-plum, is one of the few plum varieties that can be dried without severe fermentation. Dried fruits became staples in American grocery stores. Couchman, in his *Sunsweet Story* explains, "Boarding houses everywhere in the country made dried prunes a standard dessert a good part of the year." Henry Wheatley was one of the earliest Napans to grow prunes; he emigrated from England in 1892 and bought 50 acres of land just north of Napa. The income from the prune harvest allowed him to purchase 40 more acres by 1902.

Although orchard owners tried to hire local people to pick the trees, they debated among themselves about whether they could use exclusively white men at harvest or if they should employ Chinese workers. Steven Stoll writes, "The Indians and 'bindle stiffs' did not disappear with the end of mission farming and decline of bonanza wheat." They moved into the orchards, joined by thousands of Chinese miners driven out of the gold fields. The work of the orchard, including pruning, irrigating, picking, and packing, could not be mechanized. It remained a labor-hungry business and only a large and mobile labor force could move fruit from tree to packing house. Even small fruit orchards were often too large for a family to tend themselves. Stoll writes,

"Cheap labor emerged from the nature of the crops themselves as the only solution that growers could imagine for how to gather the harvest at a profit to themselves." Arguments to bar Chinese fruit workers were met by testimonials about their excellence as irrigators, pruners, and cultivators. Growers discovered that, because they had more job prospects, white workers would not work as cheaply as Chinese men, so they used newspapers to call women and children from across the state to come for a few weeks of picking. They tried recruiting men from the Midwest to come to California, hiring speakers to talk up the state with illustrated lectures of the California orchard. In spite of their efforts, young men would not cross the continent for what Stoll calls "the shallow promise of $2.00 a day in a vineyard."

Napa was thus a multicultural city from the very beginning. In addition to the indigenous and *Californio* families already in the town, Chinese families began to establish a community in the neighborhood that now encircles the Cinedome Theater. The Chinese community grew slowly but steadily; at its height, it had 500 people. Sam Brannan had recruited Chinese men from the province of Canton to help lay the Napa Valley Railroad and work in the quicksilver mines in Pope Valley. Vallejo's old Rancho Suscol, two miles south of Napa, was quarried for basalt rock and Chinese workers were hired to set dynamite charges and clear rubble from shafts. Many were killed or maimed in mining accidents and there are Chinese grave sites at Tulocay Cemetery, which document numerous deaths from this period. General Vallejo's home in Sonoma had a separate bunkhouse for his Chinese servants, and many wealthy San Franciscans who bought country property in Napa County relied extensively on the services of Chinese men who worked for them.

Napa's "Chinatown" consisted of rows of low wooden buildings between Napa Creek and the Napa River. By 1900, there were five Chinese laundries and three Chinese general stores. The two-story Joss House, or Taoist Temple, was both a spiritual and social center. Chan Wa Jack, who arrived in the 1870s, helped provide an altar for the Joss House, where sandalwood candles burned and peanut oil fueled glass lanterns. The hand-carved altar arrived in Napa on a sailing ship in 1860 along with a wooden scroll reading, "Your blessings are spread out to embrace us all." Two hundred Chinese men worked at the Sawyer Tannery; they added hand-carved pieces to decorate the altar.

The Chinese community also established a steam laundry, a barbershop, and a grocery store. A red-uniformed Chinese band performed at funerals and New Year's festivals. An opium pipe repairman had his own shop where the pipes were made of hollow bamboo with ivory mouthpieces. In 1898 Wa Jack came back to Napa from Weaverville (where he had married a Chinese bride) with his three-year-old son Shuck

Chan. Shuck Chan later went to China to marry a mail-order bride, came back to Napa in 1932, and opened a business on First Street called the Lai Hing Company, which offered Chinese nuts, candies, and other delicacies.

Attitudes toward the Chinese ranged from curiosity to hostility. This comment from The *San Francisco Post* was written in 1878 about "The Chinese of Napa County":

> Fifty men are employed in raising and peddling vegetables from the various Chinese Gardens, of which there are three in Napa. These Mongols pay a ridiculously small amount of revenue to the government in the shape of property taxes. They live mainly on rice, dried meats (which are imported) and vegetables, which they raise themselves. They patronize the white merchants but little. Now bring in the same number of Caucasians who would come to make homes. Mark the difference: 700 white men means at least three hundred families, who would live in respectable houses, patronize the carpenters, masons, furniture dealers, grocers, butchers, merchants and schools. . . . This would prove vastly more efficient to us than the present incubus of heathens who only weigh us down.

In 1860, Chinese children were forbidden from attending school in California, but in Napa this law was not strictly enforced. However, in St. Helena where anti-Chinese columns were published in the *St. Helena Star*, sticks and stones were thrown at the children. The Chinese Exclusion Act, passed in 1882 by the California Legislature, was an attempt to regulate the immigration of Chinese into California. As a result, most of the 18,000 Chinese men already in California, who had come over to work in mining and later built railroads and harvested orchards, were never able to marry or have families. After the act, the number of new Chinese workers declined.

By 1880 a new opportunity emerged for some Napa residents when the largest asylum in California was built just outside of the city. Originally, those considered mentally ill in California were put on a ship in San Francisco Bay, but eastern reformers such as Dorothea Dix and Horace Mann began advocating for enlightened treatment of the mentally ill. The establishment of the Napa Asylum was part of a national movement to create a kind of sanctuary for those considered to be unacceptable for mainstream society. As Joseph Amato explains:

> The less benign part of its mission was to incarcerate those whom society could not dare or bear to have around. Government, having defined the nation's borders and defeated the troublesome native peoples, sought a

lawful and healthy society. It set its institutional seines across the rivers of peoples pouring into the state, with the rough goal of ensnaring and removing criminals, disobedient adolescents, inebriates, and the insane.

The first asylum was built in 1850 in Stockton, but was overcrowded by the mid-1860s. California Governor Haight commissioned Dr. Edmond Wilkins to choose a model and Wilkins recommended the "moral treatment program" as the basis for a proposed new institution. Numerous communities lobbied to be the site of a new state hospital. Napa was selected for its climate, its access to the river, and the low cost of land. The area purchased included a wharf on the Napa River, a siding at the railroad tracks, and a duck ranch. Promoters exploited the similarities between California and Italy and named the location of the asylum Imola, which became an adjacent section of the town of Napa.

Construction began on the Napa State Asylum in 1873 on land previously owned by Cayetano Juarez and T.H. Thompson. The asylum opened its doors in 1876 and was described by the *Overland Monthly* as "one of the finest of these public institutions of the United States." Eventually, it housed 600 patients and had its own laundry, bakery, water supply, lumber yard, and mortuary. It manufactured coal gas on its property for lighting. The gothic building had seven towers, resembling a castle, and was a local landmark. The "Castle" had a center building with an office, library, and staff apartments. In the rear was an amusement hall, a drugstore, trunk room (for the patients' luggage), dining rooms, and a kitchen. An underground railroad transported meals and laundry between the 12 different wards.

The patients were treated with occupational therapy, which consisted of participation in farming, housekeeping, food service, and building maintenance. This "moral treatment" aimed to give the patient fresh air and access to the outdoors. It was believed that nature had great healing powers, and so vast gardens were developed on the grounds of the asylum. It had a prize-winning dairy herd and orchards that ran all the way down to the river. The first patient, admitted in 1875, was listed as a "drunkard." Many of those admitted were alcoholics and stayed about three months. Joseph Amato explains that patients in the early asylums "were sorted according to the period's primitive psychological structures, which merged prejudices, morality, philosophy, and the new science of psychology in odd combinations."

While some Californians were sentenced to the Napa Asylum, others immigrated to Napa and opened businesses. Jewish immigrants included Freedman Levinson, who opened a general store on Main Street, and Julius Salomonson, who originally sold dried goods and clothing and later entered the lumber business. By 1860, Max

Begelspecker had opened Star Bakery on First Street, which he ran until 1890. B.F. Winkler was a jeweler with a store above the Napa Hotel on Main Street, and Solomon Cohen sold goods "at New York prices" at his shop on First Street between Main and Brown.

Herman Schwartz opened a hardware store in Napa in 1870. According to Louis Ezettie, Schwartz told his customers, "Doing my own work [roofing, tinning, and plumbing], I can do it cheaper than anyone can." He sold stoves, glass, and fruit cans "at San Francisco prices," as well as agricultural equipment, making it a gathering place for farmers and fishermen. His brother Joseph opened a shop he called "The City of Paris" and built an old Victorian house, one of the few with indoor plumbing in 1890, on the northeast corner of Oak and Franklin. Other leading citizens built houses on Coombs, Randolph, School, and Church Streets. Max Schwartz opened a cigar and liquor store on Main Street near his brothers, and sometimes the entire block near the Opera House was called "The Schwartz Block."

Charlie Levinson, son of Freedman, joined forces with Abe Strauss and opened a clothing store specializing in men's wear. Charlie's brother Joe became a pharmacist and operated Levinson's Pharmacy on Main and First for many decades, frequently bartering his goods for services and earning the nickname "Pills." Charlie Levinson was a founding member of the local Native Sons chapter, while Freedman Levinson and Julius Solomonson joined the independent order of Odd Fellows, Napa Lodge #18, established in 1853.

Like most American towns in the late nineteenth century, Napans established a number of social clubs for both men and women. These included organizations advocating Prohibition and women's suffrage. Groups like the Women's Christian Temperance Union supported both, arguing that alcoholism destroyed family life and that only women could end the scourge of drink by helping turn out the vote for Prohibition. Napa College, a private school that was run by the Methodist Church, had a College Temperance Club, organized in 1884, with both male and female members.

The campaign for Women's Suffrage traveled to Napa in 1896. Susan B. Anthony, at the age of 76, spoke to enthusiastic crowds throughout Napa County. San Francisco was the seat of the California Women's Movement, which was campaigning for men to vote in suffrage for women. Delegates to Women's Suffrage meetings wore campaign badges of silky yellow, the official color of the suffrage movement.

Early *Napa Register* articles describe the local suffrage conference that was held a month after Anthony's visit, on the weekend of May 27, 1896, at the Opera House. Electa Burnell Hartson was elected president of the Political Equality Club. Mrs. Tays spoke of the "injustice of the present situation." Mrs. Mills explained the purpose of the suffrage movement and her optimism about the California Ballot Measure. She believed that "the anti's are in the minority in California; California has such excellent men; and the press in California favors equal suffrage." Mrs. Grant then spoke of examples of women throughout the world who had held political office and made a difference. Mrs. B.F. Taylor stated, "We cannot claim that our Constitution is of the people, for the people and by the people when one half of them are disenfranchised." The next day, the Reverend Anna Howard Shaw spoke. Along with Susan B. Anthony, Shaw had been working to get the vote for women for more than 40 years.

The Equal Suffrage ballot measure of 1896 failed by a large margin, due to lobbying by alcoholic beverage associations. "Considering the city's powerful saloon and liquor interests; its population dominance in the state; and the myth that voting women would shut down the liquor lobby, it was no wonder that the 1896 Suffrage Amendment failed," historian Mae Silver concludes. When California women won the suffrage battle in 1911, some of those important votes came from the prune farmers of Napa, whose wives, daughters, or sisters had attended that meeting in the Opera House in 1896.

Chapter Five

"YOUNG MAN, COME WEST TO NAPA TO START A FACTORY"

So what did I learn? That there may be powerful imagery in the most modest life, and the possibility of richness, as well.

      –John Baskin, *New Burlington: The Life and Death of an American Village*

In the early part of the twentieth century, Napa continued to grow. The first library was built, an electric railroad provided transportation, and students published their first yearbooks at Napa High. Immigrant communities thrived and new factories opened. Women won the right to vote, with the help of rural Californians.

The first library was opened on May 2, 1901. Schools closed early to allow 1,000 Napans to help lay the cornerstone at the Goodman Library First Street. George Goodman gave the library to the town after he made his banking fortune. He was known as a sweet man; his great-great granddaughter Clair Wickens recalled that he always walked to the First Presbyterian church on Sundays to give his horse a rest. Goodman erected a marble plaque in the entry hall of the library that read: "God and my Mother." The library had a men's billiard parlor, a book section, and a women's and children's tea room, because as Goodman told the *Napa Daily Journal*, "For the past thirty years, I have often noticed ladies from the county, particularly celebration and circus days, standing about the streets looking very tired, with no place where they might go to rest except to the hotels."

Every year Napa's volunteer firefighters had a Fourth of July parade. Chief Charles Otterson, born at the Mission Dolores Hotel in 1868 in San Francisco, started out as a railroad construction worker and came to Napa in 1905. He took charge of the electric car barns and became a building inspector after the 1906 earthquake. Otterson was appointed Napa's first fire chief that same year and served until 1943.

Most Napans did not own cars, but an electric train was built in 1905 that eventually traveled all the way up the valley, providing reliable transportation and steady employment. The day the electricity was connected for train operation, Napa's Mayor J.A. Fuller announced, "Napa for half a century has been slumbering in a Rip Van Winkle sleep but she has awakened at last." A great banquet was held by the 20,000 Club of Vallejo to celebrate the new railroad station next to the Vallejo ferry.

"Young Man, Come West to Napa to Start a Factory"

The first chartered electric train brought 55 officers and sailors from Mare Island, along with "several ladies and a ten piece band." The band gave a public concert at the Napa courthouse. By 1907, the electric railroad had a special round trip for Vallejo women wanting to work at the canning company in East Napa; and tickets were only 15¢. The first attempt to organize the employees of the electric railway occurred in 1909 when the president of the California Federation of Labor, A.M. Thompson, met with railroad supervisor McIntyre. Railroad historian Ira Swett explains, "Although the company was paying its electrical employees about one dollar per day less than union scale, McIntyre was not friendly to the plan to unionize his electrical employees."

A Napa County pamphlet published at the turn of the century proclaimed, "There is work for men and women here. Young man, come west! Come west to Napa to start a factory." Many factories were in fact opened in these years. The California Glove Company, which had opened in 1876, eventually employed 500 people in two factories making work gloves, driving gloves, and ladies' fine dress gloves. Former employees of the California Glove Company then started their own business, Napa Glove Company, in 1910. Cameron Shirt Company opened in 1901 and made one hundred work shirts in a day.

With a population of 5,000 people, Napa had only a few telephones and one operator, Mary Stoddard. When Stoddard left in 1900 to take a position with Sawyer Tannery, the *Napa Daily Journal* urged citizens to be patient "until the new operator becomes accustomed to the names of the subscribers." Sawyer Tannery bought deer skins for 38¢ a pound in the summer, and in winter they were 28¢. Wet, salted cowhides were 9¢ a pound, and calves were 10¢. Wet, salted horse hides were $2, with colts going for 50¢. When World War I created a shortage of chemicals, Sawyer went into the hills of Napa and found chrome ore, from which they made dichromate of soda, the chief element used to tan leather. Emmanuel Manasse invented new methods of tanning sheep skin and buck skin; with his help in 1909, Sawyer Tannery developed Nap-A-Tan Waterproof Leather and Napa Patent Leather.

On the outskirts of town, dairy farming was widespread. One major farm was the Ambrosia Dairy, developed by William Watt, who came to Napa in 1906 and purchased part of Salvador Vallejo's land grant. He began to manufacture ice cream and produced thousands of gallons every summer. Eventually, he distributed many kinds of dairy products. Watt's Creamery wagons traveled daily through Napa, Sonoma, and Solano counties. One of his main sources of milk was from Manuel Almada, whose dairy farm in Soscol was on the land that had once belonged to Mariano Vallejo.

NAPA

Within the town itself, Henry Wigger told interviewer Laura Thomas:

> Everybody had their own milk cows, chickens, and vegetable gardens.
> Frank Noyes had a cow up there where the Bank of America on First Street
> is now. Starting at the corner of Pearl and Main, Louie Zaro had a store,
> vegetable and groceries. There was the Napa City Bakery owned by the
> Stoll family; Bernard's Butcher Shop was on the right hand side going
> south, in the left hand side was the post office. Keig's Shoe Store went all
> the way from Main to Brown Street; you could get anything you wanted in
> fine footwear. Across the creek was China Town. We used to go there and
> get a dried abalone for a nickel.

Two other much loved downtown businesses were Carol Inman's Cycle Shop and
Bryant's Candy Store. The cycle shop provided both sales and service to groups like
the Eagle Cycling Club. Ed Bryant opened the candy store at 81 Main Street where
he developed his own candy recipes. His granddaughter Diane Adams treasures her
grandfather's notebook, "filled with his secrets for creating mouthwatering treats,"
according to interviewer Rebecca Yerger. After Bryant married Emma Hedley, they
moved to 1129 First Street; their children grew up at the candy store and remember
tasting treats such as taffies, fudges, and French creams.

Napa High School opened in 1897. In 1910, the faculty included Mr. Glen Allen,
principal and chemistry and geography teacher; Miss Dora Martin, Latin teacher; Miss
Cora Gaensch, who instructed German and algebra; Miss E. Grace Ward, who taught
history and drawing; and Miss Ida Cowley, English and arithmetic teacher. The 1910
yearbook, *the Napanee*, features an advertisement for Herman Schwartz's Hardware
Store, advertising 150 different pairs of pocket knives and "beautiful lamps for gas, oil
or electric." On the inside back cover is an ad for the Napa Coffee Club, declaring "free
reading and rest room, a complete dinner for $.25 on Second Street opposite the Court
House." In an eerie resemblance to more modern times, the student editors wrote:

> The feeling of "I don't care" and "What's the use" is written on the faces
> of many who pass back and forth through these halls. They come to school
> in the morning, recite their lessons, and go home at 3:30; unless, perchance,
> they receive a special invitation to remain later. Day after day, this is
> repeated: coming, reciting, going. That is all. That is all there is to their
> High School Life. They do not seem to consider themselves, in any way, a
> part of the school life.

"Young Man, Come West to Napa to Start a Factory"

The Napanee of 1911 was edited by Pearl Gifford. The class colors were green and white, and the class flower was a white carnation. At graduation, Senior Class President Dorothy Coombs wrote:

> Many things we were to learn in that queer brown building with its falling plaster, cracking floors and narrow stairs. With this scenery we played our part for two eventful years. At first the boys and girls were separated, for better or worse, probably the latter, for the order did not seem to improve.

This yearbook advertises Joseph Levinson as "The Leading Druggist," and The Popular Dining Room on 13-15 Main Street as "The Leading Restaurant of Napa." Unadvertised in the yearbooks was the fact that both sides of Clinton Street were lined with houses of prostitution, possibly as many as 20. When East Napa flooded in 1909, some of the women went out and swam in the floodwaters. When the city granted liquor licenses to these businesses, citizens wrote to complain not about the business, but about the liquor. Charles Johnson, who wrote an article for the local paper on the red light district in 1963, says that some houses catered to judges and bankers, lonely immigrant workers, and poor white men:

> The girls, usually well-dressed, were often seen alone or in pairs walking down Main Street on shopping tours. They rarely if ever used the street to make appointments. They were of course never seen in bars or other low places, which in those days were strictly reserved for men.

Johnson calls prostitution "a necessary function of society like barbering or horseshoeing" and notes that community leaders "thought nothing of parking their easily identifiable buggies in front of the Clinton Street houses." Mae Howard was one of the most famous madams, in an era when women ran prostitution and police were often tolerant. But in 1913, when the police raided Chinatown, the *Napa Journal* described the suspects as "two white devotees at the shrine of Madjoun (the opium god), also seven 'Chinks' assiduously trying to get rid of the 'yen yen' (craving for opium)." This report suggests some interracial contact not otherwise documented, as well as the type of racist language used to describe the Chinese.

Women continued to work for full citizenship, in the hope that the female vote would raise wages and end prostitution. In 1911 suffrage was again on the ballot, but this time it had support from the socialist movement newspaper *The Call*, edited by John Spreckels. Spreckels was one son of the sugar king Claus Spreckels; his brother

NAPA

Adolph raised race horses behind what is now the River Park Shopping Center. The College Equal Suffrage League campaigned in a special car named the Blue Liner, in which they toured California. Mae Silver says, "Trimmed like a pet horse, the car sported yellow streamers and was especially appealing to men."

After the election, both leading San Francisco newspapers, the *Examiner* and the *Chronicle*, declared suffrage defeated, but *The Call* reminded readers that the vote had not yet been counted and predicted that suffrage would win with 4,000 votes. In the final tally, it won with 3,587 votes, with farmers in counties like Napa making the difference. In gratitude for the suffrage victory, the league wrote an "Ode to the Farmers Who Voted a Majority for Us":

> But from the strength of the hills
> Men's voices hailed us;
> God bless our farmer-folk,
> Scarce a man failed us!

One of the women to benefit from suffrage was Ruth Bickford, whose yearbooks and diaries document both a personal and a public history. Her father Elmer Bickford moved to Napa in 1886 and eventually became president of First National Bank on First Street. He and wife Ada Easterby had a son, Robert, in 1904 and daughter Ruth in 1907. The Bickford house was at 1303 Jefferson Street, where Elmer Bickford garaged one of the town's first automobiles, an Oldsmobile, in October 1904. Bickford co-founded the Boy Scouts of Napa. When he took the boy scouts bird watching at Tulocay Cemetary, Big and Little Trancas, McKenzie's Nursery on Waterworks Road, and the bridge west of Union Station, they recorded 76 different species.

Ruth Bickford grew up next door to best friend Mildred Pearch, and Ruth and Millie wrote letters to silent movie star Rudolph Valentino in a tree behind their houses. Mildred attended Washington Street School in 1914. At the age of 94 she could still remember the teachers, recalling, "Miss A.L. Maxwell taught first grade and Miss Ames, second grade. . . . Most of the teachers were old maiden ladies. After they married they had to leave teaching. Most of the teachers were boarders. Some of the homes down by Fuller Park became permanent boarding houses."

In her interview with Rebecca Yerger, Pearch recalls spending most of the day on reading, writing, spelling, and penmanship. She describes writing with a fountain pen as "quite tricky using those wobbly glass jars of ink on your desk. If you push your book into your desk too hard, out pops the ink well, making quite a mess." She remembers walking home at noon where her mother always had a hot lunch waiting.

"Young Man, Come West to Napa to Start a Factory"

The Italian children brought their lunches to school because, "I guess their mothers had to work." Millie's mother Agnes was the truant officer.

East Napa was populated by Italians, with cousins Nelly Lagorio and Uriglia Magini growing up in what had been Juarez's Tulocay Grant and Napa's "Little Italy." Italian houses all had two kitchens, one in the basement and another on the first floor in case of flooding. Nelly's father ran a trading post for the few remaining indigenous people in Napa. She married Dave Cavagnaro, whose father had opened the Brooklyn Hotel. Dave and Nelly took over the trading post, but when the indigenous population continued to decline they ran the Brooklyn Hotel. The old trading post came to be known as "Dave's Place." Lou Guisto told interviewer Laura Thomas:

> I was born in the Brooklyn Hotel, next to the railroad tracks. My mom ran the hotel; my dad worked for the railroad and then he raised potatoes off Coombsville Road. They were boarding hotels for Italian people. Most of the men didn't marry. They would get together and sing and play Bocce Ball. Our brother, Dave, was a grand man. He used to help the Italians a lot. When he married Nelly Lagorio, they ran the hotel together. Every room had boot jacks. They wore leather boots in those days and you needed the jack to get them off.

Dave Cavagnaro would become the "unofficial Mayor" of East Napa, as well as a circus roustabout in the decades to come, while the restaurant that his family founded at the Depot would become the most historic and beloved eatery in town.

Chapter Six

BOYSENBERRIES AND

BASEBALL GLOVES

Simultaneously, the object of the most profound feelings, the subject of the greatest nostalgia, and the topic for a lifetime of rethinking, home is local historians' measure of every other place.

—Joseph Amato, *Rethinking Home*

From 1915 to 1930, Napa was the site of multiple inventions. The microphone, the boysenberry, and the Italian dish "malfatti" were all conceived here. Napa men were drafted to fight in World War I—and some participated in resistance to that war. Napa became a center of dried fruit production, and developed the Farm Bureau and the 4-H club. Sawyer Tannery was central to the local economy, and Napa High and Fuller Park became the focus of memories for teenagers and children respectively.

A spectacular event occurred on F Street in 1915. *Napa Register* reporter Phyllis King described it as "the sounds of music and voices heard throughout the city seeming to come from the heavens. Many thought the world was coming to an end and scrambled for cover." Peter Jensen and Edwin Pridham had moved to Napa from San Francisco in 1911 to work on a new type of telephone receiver. Jensen recalled, "San Francisco businessman Dick O'Connor sent us out in the country where we could work undisturbed." They bought their bungalow at 1606 F Street for $2,500. When they developed the "dynamic loud speaking telephone," Jenson wrote, "It was the first 'great voice' which became the voice of public speakers, the voice of film, and last but not least, the voice of radio!" Jensen and Pridham entertained their neighbors by playing records over the loudspeaker all that summer. They left Napa in 1916 to establish a factory in Oakland, naming their company Magnavox, the Latin word for "Great Voice."

In 1916 workers on the steamboats between San Francisco and Vallejo went on strike. The Monticello Steamship Company operated the steamers between San Francisco and Vallejo, which then connected to the electric train to Napa. The Steamboat Owners Association refused to grant a pay raise from $50 to $55 a month, and to reduce the work day from 17 to 13 hours. When the strike began, non-union crews (ex-convicts and men from the Thiele Detective Agency) were hired to keep the boats running. Stevedores and longshoremen joined the strike, closing down the entire San Francisco waterfront; the San Francisco Chamber of Commerce organized a committee to condemn the strikers. The strike continued off and on until 1917, when the workers received a 10 percent increase in pay, but lost the fight for a "union shop."

In 1917 America entered the First World War. Napa had been given a quota of 134 inductees, based on a random lottery of eligible men. In June 1917, attorneys Frank Silva and Charles Trower drove through the county, encouraging men ages 18–45 to enlist. The Napa Band rode on the electric train, also promoting enlistment. District Attorney Frank Coombs closed all businesses so that citizens could say goodbye once eligible men were found. The Napa Band escorted these soldiers to the Southern Pacific Depot. At the farewell rally, a speech later described as "anti-German, anti-pacifist, and anti-IWW" was given by Judge McLaughlin of Sacramento.

The IWW (International Workers of the World) was a radical union that had been organizing workers since 1905. Their members believed that the war would be a tragic waste of lives. In 1917 Congress passed the Espionage Act, which imprisoned people for up to 20 years if they spoke or wrote against the war. Teachers who opposed the war were fired from colleges, and the first woman in Congress, Jeanette Rankin, lost her seat for her anti-war position. Nationally, 900 people went to jail under the Espionage Act; in Napa, George Peterson, a member of the IWW, was arrested. Perry Schriver, a German immigrant staying at the Connor Hotel at the corner of Third and Main, was jailed because of what the *Napa Daily Journal* called "treasonable utterances." Harry Sawyer of Martinez was featured on the front page of the *Journal* stating that "America has no business in this war." He was escorted by guards to Angel Island.

The *Napa Daily Journal* reported that the Farm Labor Committee of the state recommended to Governor Stephens that if the law failed to protect people from the IWW, "Citizens should take them by the neck and drown them in the river." At the farewell rally for inductees, Judge Gesford concluded his remarks with the opinion that "seditious [anti-war] people should be shot."

By 1918 the public was becoming more aware of the loss of life inherent in wartime. The *Napa Daily Journal* wrote that President Wilson was about to draw the names again from "the big glass bowl holding the fate of the nation's 18–45 [year old] human war material." When the war ended, all of Napa closed down as a celebration exploded with bells, bands, sirens, and fire crackers. Local historians Denzil and Jenny Verardo wrote, "Perhaps the most joyful group were the sixty-three men who were to be inducted into the United States Army at the courthouse that day, but who had their orders cancelled due to the Armistice." Returning veterans included Louis Guisto, who had played professional baseball for Philadelphia before the war. After being gassed in France, he had to leave the team.

The intolerance that accompanied World War I reverberated into the Twenties. In 1923, 200 Ku Klux Klan members gathered by moonlight in a field near the state hospital. Two thousand spectators watched them ignite a 20-foot cross and initiate 100 new members.

The previous year, California's Department of Institutions had changed the clinical term for insanity to mental illness. Although the asylum was now called Napa State Hospital, treatment remained the same. Journalist Jane Smith describes a neighbor, Abbey Halteman, who lived next door to her on Second Street, and who worked as a nurse at the Napa State hospital:

> She drove a sporty Ford and sat up high in the driver's seat, erect as a queen in her carriage. She wore her silver hair coiled in a bun on top of her head held by tortoise shell hair pins and her nurse's cap on top of her bun. . . . I admired her beautiful working clothes, the long sleeved black and white striped uniform covered by a starched white apron, white shoes and the cap. She worked every day at the hospital, a turreted mysterious place where the corridors of the main building were hushed, where the floors shined with wax, and the waiting room was graced with green potted palms . . . the very picture of a place of rest and healing, but a madhouse none the less.

Smith recalls the ball games attended by Napa townspeople where they would watch the patients caged in the fenced-in yards. She writes: "The nurses were white clad figures of authority that had to rely upon their own strength and the hospital routines of eating, bathing and dressing and a little socializing to soothe the sufferings of the mentally ill. . . . People like Abbey Halteman were the guardian angels of the mad."

The patients worked in the dairies and orchards; Napa had hundreds of acres of the oldest black walnut trees in California. In the early twentieth century, American farmers organized cooperatives to stabilize prices and promote consumption of dried fruit. Growers decided to develop a state-wide cooperative, and prune farmer Henry Wheatley represented Napa County in the Growers Central Committee. In 1917 when the cooperative was incorporated, Wheatley, along with Harry Dunlap of Yountville, represented District 2. Arrangements were made with 45 packers statewide, including Ralph Butler of the Napa Fruit Company, to receive and pack the 1917 crops.

By 1923 the *San Francisco Chronicle* wrote: "Napa County farmers believe in cooperative marketing" and described Napa pears as reaching "a fine state of perfection." Within this crop one-third were canned, one-third dried, and one-third shipped green. Ninety percent of Napa prune growers were members of an association, as were the pear and cherry growers. The biggest employer during the fruit picking season was the Napa Fruit Company, which became famous for its "Napa Pack." The *Chronicle* added, "A great bulk of prunes are dried in the sun, but of late years the dehydrator had come rapidly to the fore, and Napa becomes the third county in the state for the number of its dehydrators." Locally grown fruits and nuts were sold all over the country. William Fisher installed a fruit dryer on his property near Union Station at Trancas where other fruit growers would bring their stock.

Herman Baade, an agriculture teacher at Napa High School, began to give lectures in 1914 at the Grange, which was both a building and a farmers association. Baade used a bulletin from the University of California at Berkeley that gave advice to farmers. Early settler Nathan Coombs, who was by then the district attorney, "got excited about the idea of creating a county farm agent," according to John Wagenknecht, former director of the University of California Cooperative Extension. Coombs organized 12 to 15 farm centers where farmers met to learn farming and to share ideas. The centers were one-story buildings located in Browns Valley, Mount George, Carneros, Coombsville, Salvador, Soscol, and Oak Knoll According to the *Chronicle* of 1923, these centers allowed people to get acquainted "in a way that is pleasant and often produces life-long friendships."

Napa was one of the first five counties in the state to have farm centers, which eventually became the Farm Bureau. Farm advisors oversaw the transition in Napa from grain, oats, and pasture to horticulture and eventually viticulture. 4-H clubs were created out of concern over the isolation of rural children, and in an effort to teach citizenship and leadership. Ruby Flowers, a home economist, was an early leader of the Women's Auxiliary to the Farm Centers, where women learned to cover lampshades, stuff mattresses, and can with pressure cookers. University of California Cooperative Extension initially worked closely with the Farm bureaus throughout the state, but decided to cut off its official relationship in the 1920s, when the bureaus became industry lobbyists.

NAPA

Many Napa residents look back fondly to their lives in the fields and orchards in the Twenties. Olamae Wade came to Napa in 1924 when she was three years old. All her family's possessions were on the back of a truck after a flood had washed their house down a river in Texas. They pitched a tent at Gardner's Auto Camp along Napa Creek. "Chinatown" still stood across First Street, and Olamae remembers sneaking out to visit it with her brothers and sisters. In 1928 her family rented a farmhouse in Browns Valley where prune orchards stretched "as far as you could see," and where she and her brothers picked prunes. She attended Browns Valley School, which was a one-room eight-grade school with 26 students and a wood-burning stove. Olamae remembers skating down Browns Valley Road into downtown Napa without fear of being hit by a car.

Ruth Raider, who would become one of Napa's most beloved growers, moved to town in 1923 to join her uncle who was an "orchardist" for the asylum. Ruth worked on a ranch in the summer for a disabled World War I veteran, where she pitched hay and picked fruit. She attended the University of California at Berkeley, doing housework to pay her tuition of $25 a semester, and bought her first motorcycle in 1929 for $10—a signal that she would always be an unconventional woman.

Rudolph Boysen, a farmer and amateur horticulturalist, invented the boysenberry in 1924 while living on Third Avenue. He combined pollen from a blackberry and "some other kind of berry." When he left for Anaheim in 1925, he took six vines with him, which he planted in an orange grove. His new berry was 50 percent bigger and juicier than the blackberry, but no one was interested until 1932, when a scientist from the U.S. Department of Agriculture came to Anaheim. The scientist found Walter Knott, who ran a berry truck garden. The two of them tracked down Boysen, who led them to the orange grove where the vines were half dead, on the verge of extinction. Out of those vines, Knott's Berry Farm was created.

Industry continued to flourish. Basalt Rock Company was founded on September 15, 1924, by A.G. Streblow, who held the shovel himself while Ed Brovelli did the bookkeeping and stenography. Such was the demand for the crushed stone that an aerial tramway was built from the quarry to the Napa River, where it was dumped on wooden barges and taken to Sacramento or San Francisco. In 1926 Sawyer was the first tannery west of Chicago to produce patent leather. One year later, Sawyer developed chromed tan leather, which was perfect for baseball and softball gloves; they also developed leather for welder's gloves.

South Franklin Street, a couple of blocks from the tannery, was a neighborhood of tanners, paperhangers, stevedores, and river men. Edna and Rita Guisti grew up on

Levee Street (now called Riverside Drive). They went barefoot all summer, wearing ragged cotton dresses with bloomers underneath. They climbed the big oak on Oak Street, which had a big rope swing over the river. Although Fire Chief Otterson threatened to send any of the children he saw swimming in the river to the Children's Detention Home, he never did. The river was still clear; carp would come to the surface and children tried to spear them with willow branches to sell to Napa's remaining Chinese families. Lin Weber writes:

> The big whistle on top of the water tower at the Sawyer Tannery was one of life's regulators for children like Edna and Rita, and for their parents, as well. It blew every day of the year at 6 a.m., 12 noon and 4 p.m. Sometimes the overly loud fire siren had a special code that advertised the part of town the fire was in, so anyone who wanted could go and watch. A common cause of fires during Prohibition was the explosion of home-made stills.

On the northern side of downtown, banker's daughter Ruth Bickford kept a diary. On April 16, 1924, she wrote: "Helped serve tea at meeting with Mildred [Pearch]. Wore Linen." After she met her high-school sweetheart and future husband, Burr Northrop, she stopped writing. Ruth's 1924 yearbook describes the senior class this way:

> G. Morris, nickname: "George"; Appearance: Vacant; Famous Saying: Oh Gee; Hobby: Doing Nothing; Opinion of Self: "Gee, I'm good looking." C. Myers, nickname: "Casty"; Appearance: Meekly inconspicuous; Famous Saying: "Oh, for goodness sakes!"; Hobby: Being Nice; Opinion of Self: "I am an S student!" W. Galbraith, nickname: "Walt," Appearance: censored; favorite saying: "My Gosh!" Hobby: 'loving 'em all'; Opinion of self: 'I can outrun any speed cop.' "

After graduating, Ruth was able to attend Cal Berkeley by taking the green cars of the electric train. to Vallejo. She then boarded a ferry across the Carquinez Straits to Crockett, where the electric train whisked her all the way to campus. The 1925 *Napanee* describes what other graduates were doing. Ruth Daly was teaching at John Shearer School (John Shearer had been a classroom teacher in 1900 and had introduced the idea of elementary school graduation), while Lois Daughty was "at home" in Napa, as was Wayne Douglas. Eugenia Donahue was employed at JC

Penney's, Blanche Lui was at La Mode Beauty Parlor, Verona Steere at the Napa Post Office, while Muriel Van Pelt was "Mrs. Kenneth Johnson" in Vallejo. Barbara Chisholm was the assistant cashier at the Hippodrome Theater and the Edwards sisters were both attending Napa Business College. Erler Frisch was at Keig Shoe Company, Lucille Wilson was clerking at Woolworth's, David Wright worked for Abe Strauss, and Robert Manasse at Sawyer Tanning Company. Twenty-five years into the new century, Napa's youth found employment in local businesses; the only surviving site is the Second Street Post Office.

The City of Napa had purchased 10 acres of orchards in 1905 for $12,000. The land was cleared for the first city park, designed by J.H. Chalmers. In 1919, the park was renamed after Mayor Jack Fuller, who had presided over its purchase. Jane Smith grew up at 1915 Second Street, a home that she visited recently to find "ghosts still sitting in the chairs." She described for the *Register* her birthday celebrations in Fuller Park:

> I remember my peach Crepe De Chine dress, white silk stocking stationed by a garter just below the knee and black patent leather Mary Jane shoes, with button straps. Bangs trimmed for the occasion by Mr. Lui, at Lui's beauty shop in Main Street. Cake and candles and ice cream from Modern Dairy made the day. Presents, too. Writing paper for little ladies, pin the donkey on a tree.

She remembers there being only one policeman, and "he went home at night." Of her debt to J.H. Chalmers, Smith writes, "for all my pleasant hours spent listening to the trees whisper. The bottle tree, the gorgeous gingko, purple leaf plum, Chinese pistachio, swamp cypress, the redwoods, the huge Christmas tree, lighted every year, the signal for Christmas to begin in Napa."

Jane and cousins Bob and Jackie would climb up the big cannon on the northeast corner of the park and shoot imaginary cannonballs at the motorists passing by on Jefferson Street. Smith recollects, "Little did I know that I would have to say goodbye to Bob and Jackie many years too soon . . . but they loved me all their lives, and I them, and our bonds were forged forever from our young beginnings in Fuller Park and tramping in my Aunt Flo's Browns Valley orchard and playing in the empty lot on Second Street, telling stories in the twilight."

Thomas Malloy was also born in town in 1911, but he moved to his grandmother's farm east of the river at the end of Big Ranch Road after his mother's death. He describes this area, the Duffy ranch, as "a paradise of open space, orchards, and a few settled homes." Due to fear of the 1918 and 1920 influenza epidemics, he and his brother were kept at the farm and tutored until the fourth grade, when they entered Salvador School. In 1921 Malloy's father remarried and moved the two boys back into town; they graduated from St. Johns Catholic School in 1924 and from Napa High in 1928. Malloy's first job was in 1930 at the new 500-seat State Theater on Main Street between Second and Third. He would work in the motion picture business for the rest of his life.

Chapter Seven

VANISHING PLACES:
THE DREAM BOWL AND
SHIPYARD ACRES

Local historians cherish vanishing places, and the more they cherish their subjects, the more they recognize how little others care about them, and how helpless they are to preserve them from the ravages of time. Only a handful of documents and one's own passionate efforts stake places to a crumbling bank.

–Joseph Amato, *Rethinking Home*

Napa experienced the Depression and World War II as a time of endings and beginnings. Although the cleanup of the Napa River demolished the remnants of the city's Chinatown and the opening of the Bay bridges led to the end of the electric railroad, the development of cooperative dryers enabled thousands of Napans to work year-round in the fruit industry, and the opening of movie palaces allowed citizens to dream of other worlds. Another significant beginning for Napa was the establishment of Rough Rider Clothing Factory, a large employer with a unionized work force. The unionization of other factories and stores in Napa brought dramatic improvements in wages and working conditions. The war years were a time of ending for the 54 Japanese citizens who were ordered out of Napa County, but a time of beginnings for the women who were able to work in the trades and war industries at Mare Island. The State Hospital continued to provide job opportunities for thousands of other residents, while its inmates haunted the imaginations of local townspeople. The community college was founded, the first class on Napa history was taught, and the historical society began to collect the photographs that would document the history of the town.

The end of the electric railroad and its beloved green cars began in 1929 when Southern Pacific ended its passenger line in Napa. They also cut river service from South Vallejo to Napa Junction and turned mail delivery over to the electric railroad. In 1930 Greyhound Bus Lines sought permission from the railroad commission to merge its companies in California. The expansion of Greyhound was opposed by the Napa City Council, the Napa Chamber of Commerce, and the Napa Central Labor Council. "It was the belief of these bodies that the inter-urban [electric train] had long rendered adequate dependable and comfortable transportation service," writes Ira Swett. Nevertheless, the Railroad Commission decided in favor of Greyhound.

In 1932 a fire erupted in Napa's interurban train barn. Cars were destroyed, the expensive electrical equipment was burned, and the railway seemed dead. Manager Clyde Brown laid off all 70 employees. Townspeople came to the support of the interurban, aggressively campaigning to get the electric trains back in service. Large ads were taken out in local newspapers calling for electric railway service to resume. These efforts met with little success and, by 1938, buses had successfully replaced the electric train. The building of the Bay and Golden Gate Bridges during the 1930s—what Ira Swett calls "the hangman's scaffold"—destroyed the financial success of ferries because people could no longer take the electric train to Napa after taking the ferry to Vallejo.

In the winter of 1930 Mayor Charles Trower launched a campaign to clean up the Napa River, where occasionally dead bodies were found floating. The Napa River Club's first project was to move the last seven Chinese families out of town; frequent mysterious fires between 1915 and 1930 had already forced most Chinese residents out. Their wooden dwellings were replaced by a park called "China Point."

In 1936 the Napa Chamber of Commerce told Rough Rider Clothing Factory in San Francisco that if the factory moved to Napa, the chamber would raise and donate the $40,000 needed to buy the land, a 5,000 square-foot lot between the river and railroad. Julian Weidler, who moved to Napa to set up the factory, had worked for Rough Rider while he attended college in Berkeley, financing his education with his $40-per-month salary. There were many men's clothing stores in downtown Napa eager for Rough Rider apparel, including Voorhees, Straus, Albert's, and Grossman's.

After the factory opened, boats left Lowell, Massachusetts carrying cotton and wool through the Panama Canal into the San Francisco Bay, and up the Napa River on barges to unload at the factory. Rough Rider could also ship materials on the Southern Pacific Railroad; the depot was located across the street.

Although boys graduating from Napa High could become apprentices at Mare Island, girls did not have similar job opportunities until Rough Rider came to town. Classes were offered in high school to learn sewing on power machines and eventually over 500 workers, mostly women, were employed at Rough Rider. Weidler recalls that he always had cordial relationships with his unionized employees.

The Rough Rider Cookbook was published by United Garment Workers, Local 197. It lists the unions belonging to the Napa Central Labor Council, documenting the availability of union work to Napa citizens by 1940. Bartenders, retail clerks, musicians, dried fruit packers, barbers, cleaners, carpet layers, and grain processors all belonged to trade unions. In addition, the cookbook contains a recipe for "malfatti," invented by Theresa Tamburelli, who ran the Depot Restaurant along with her husband Joseph. The Depot was across the street from Rough Rider, next to the train station and across from the Brooklyn Hotel. One evening, Theresa ran out of flour for ravioli, so she boiled up stuffing without cases and called it Malfatti, meaning "poorly made" in Italian.

Malfatti

1 quart Swiss chard or spinach, well drained, chopped, and cooked.	2 cloves garlic, chopped
	2 teaspoons parsley, chopped
1 1/2 pounds ground round	1 small onion, chopped
8 eggs	1/4 teaspoon poultry seasoning
1 cup flour	1 cup grated Italian cheese
1 quart grated bread crumbs	salt and pepper to taste

Mix all together well. If mixture is too soft, add more bread crumbs. Sprinkle flour on board. Drop teaspoon of mixture on floured board and roll into small balls. Sprinkle more flour if needed. Drop into pot of slated boiling water. Cook about 3 minutes or until they rise to top. Drain and put into bowl or platter and sprinkle with grated cheese and Italian sauce.

Italian Sauce

1 pound ground round—fried add. . .	parsley to season
	1 cup tomato sauce
1 onion	2 cups solid pack tomatoes
3 cloves garlic	1 cup mushrooms, chopped

Add one quart of water and boil slowly for 2 hours. Salt and pepper to taste.

The Great Depression did not impact Napa as badly as other parts of the country. Cecil Mathews, for example, had grown up on the family ranch on Orchard Avenue. His great-grandfather Joseph Mateus had come from Portugal and built the Lisbon Winery, known for its sherry, in 1880. When Cecil Mathews's family lost the farm during the Depression, he went on the road. He returned to town because he found work at Basalt, which enabled him to buy a prune orchard on Monticello Road for his new family home. For those who couldn't find work, the local Unemployment Relief Committee established four camps where men cut trees and sold firewood.

Vanishing Places: The Dream Bowl and Shipyard Acres

The Mare Island Naval Shipyard was a major source of employment, largely responsible for sparing Napans from the worst of the Depression. Basalt Corporation benefited from Mare Island because barges went up and down the river between them, and Basalt was invited to help build the Bay Bridge. Carol Raahauge Grant was born as a result of the activity at Mare Island. Her mother worked in an office there, took the ferry every day from Vallejo, and met the ferry owner's son, Nay Raahauge. They got married and bought a farm on Hagen Road in 1937, where they opened The Hagen Road Dairy. Their daughter Carol told stories of milking the cows, which she named Doris and Betty. Carol's family churned butter and sold milk in bottles to customers at their Hagen Dairy drive-in.

Local businesses struggled to survive, especially when traveling salesmen came to town with suitcases full of cheap merchandise. These peddlers were often arrested for selling without a license. In 1932 the *Napa Daily Journal* urged shoppers to support local businesses, arguing that "chain stores are undermining our local economic structure." By 1939 directors of the Napa Chamber of Commerce issued the statement, "It is hard to get new members because business conditions are not good, collections are slow and businesses cannot see the way to shoulder any additional expense." Rough Rider Clothing Company extended generous amounts of credit to its Bay Area customers; many acknowledged that they were saved from economic disaster by the gesture.

Not all businesses suffered during the Depression. Sawyer Tannery thrived, making woolen lining for coats and baseball gloves. The Napa Paper Box Company at Pine and Ornduff Street also combatted the downturn by making jigsaw puzzles, an affordable form of family entertainment. The staff worked overtime because of the huge demand, producing 20,000 puzzles a week.

Napans were also listening to the radio and going to movies. Although there was no local radio station in Napa until 1946, national radio programs formed an important link among American citizens. Similarly, going to the movies became a very popular pastime by 1929. Thomas Malloy remembers watching the construction of the Hippodrome Theater, which became the Fox, as he sat in Dr. C.H. Farman's dental office on the southwest corner of First and Randolph in 1920. It seated 1,500 people and had an orchestra pit with a massive pipe organ. During silent movies Malloy remembers hearing organist Eugene Brown and thinking, "he almost made the organ talk."

The Uptown opened on Third Street in 1937 with 1,200 seats and Malloy as the manager. It had a central ceiling of angels painted by muralist Dick Echeles. Malloy describes the "well-trained team of young ladies in matching uniforms" who served as usherettes. When the house was full, Malloy had an usher at every exit and was considered a "safety guy," criticized by the owners for having so many employees. To survive during the Depression, theater owners devised gimmicks to persuade the public to pay the 35¢ admission price. The most popular promotion was Bank Night, which featured a money jackpot.

In 1940 Malloy married a cashier from the theater named Dolly Farrell. "She was very adept at selling tickets and making change while keeping all the ticket prices straight. One time I walked into the box office to see if she needed some help and I noticed she had her shoes off. I then teased her that I now knew how she was so efficient because she used her toes to count." They bought a house at the corner of Yajome and K Street for $2,000. In an interview with Rebecca Yerger, Malloy recalled: "After Pearl [Harbor] was bombed it was a wild time here. The manning of Monticello Road as a look-out, the presence of Mare Island made Napans uneasy about being a potential enemy target. It was trying times, and people were looking for an outlet, to get away from things. So they went to the movies." Special morning matinees were scheduled for swing-shift workers from Mare Island and Basalt.

Owner Lawrence Borg had planned a red lobby for the Uptown, but it was toned down to salmon pink, due to the growing fear of the "Red Menace." During this period radical politics flourished across America. Although the Communist party organized in nearby Vacaville and Fairfield, they were not as active in Napa County. When an organizer left a pamphlet in a voting booth in Rutherford urging those making less than 40¢ a day to strike, Sheriff Stechter set up a vigilante committee to keep "Reds" out of the community. Two suspected communist organizers were tarred and feathered in nextdoor Sonoma County.

Thomas Malloy remembers Napa being largely Republican in the 1930s, but says that "lots of people needed help." He remembers that townspeople picked wild mustard and later, in the Forties, they grew Victory Gardens in their yards. In 1949 the Malloys bought a house on Spruce Street, where they raised their four children.

Ruth Bickford's son Bob grew up going to matinees at the Fox Theater; he recalls that every child's bike was parked unlocked at either the Fox or the Uptown on Saturday afternoons. Beautician Chris Aultman remembers going to the Fox Theater and especially the mezzanine, "I liked going up both sides, it reminded you of something really elegant. Napa was a country town, this was something really special." She also remembers the Dream Bowl, a dance hall on Kelly Road: "All our parents used to go there." Patsy Kline and Johnny Cash both performed at the Dream Bowl.

According to Chris, children loved Vichy Springs, owned by Merle and Grace Harris, which had a swimming pool open to the public. Journalist Jane Smith writes,

Vanishing Places: The Dream Bowl and Shipyard Acres

"It was nothing to walk from Second Street out to the end of Third Street, down the Silverado Trail to Monticello Road, to Vichy's, the only swimming tank in Napa, to swim all day and walk home again, pink and raw from sun burn." Some days they had to wait while the tank was filled. Smith describes Mrs. Briles who "dispensed candy bars, drinks, gum, and rented rubber bathing caps summer after summer after summer. She was judge, jury, mother, father, policeman, swimming teacher and lifeguard. A swim was $.10."

In Jane Smith's memory of those Depression summers, "There weren't that many cars. Or people. The neighborhoods were clustered close around the town. First Street on the west stopped where the orchards began. Browns Valley Road was all country, flanked by prune trees, and only a few farm houses." She remembers quiet summer days when "you watched for the tar to soften up in the street and come up bubbles. Then chewed it." There were ice chips off the union ice truck, and aroma from the Bon Ton Bakery wagon "that set the taste buds dancing." Mr. Schambacher delivered French bread twice a week. "He drove up front, round, rosy, plump, shyly smiling." Smith also remembers trapping bees and reading poems in her apple tree.

Napa was becoming an important part of the state prune industry. In 1934 the Prune Association built its first automatic bulk packing line. According to *The Sunsweet Story*, "No association development of this period was more important or more far-reaching in impact than the organization of the first cooperative dryer in Napa County." Frank Randall came up with the idea of a dehydrator that could handle 2,500 tons of fruit. John Cantoni designed the new plant with a heating chamber, a fan, and an automatic scale. Other communities (Campbell, San Jose, and Yuba City) copied the idea of a cooperative dryer. Another group of Napa growers organized the Napa Mutual Dehydrator in 1932, which operated until 1950.

The lives of many Napans like Olamae Wade were largely shaped by the prune industry. Her mother was a harvest captain for the prune farms in Browns Valley. Her father abandoned the family in 1936; they believed he had suffered amnesia from a World War I injury and just wandered away. Olamae worked at the cannery pitting maraschino cherries and also helped her mother in the orchards. She and her sisters would roller skate downtown, often going to the fire station at Second and Wilson to ask Chief Otterson for a ride home if it was too dark.

One afternoon after going to the Fox Theater, Olamae and a friend were waiting for her brother to drive them home. Instead, Archie Combellack stopped by. "He wanted to date me, but my mother said 'no, you're too young,' " Olamae describes. They were only allowed to go to the movies with both her brother and sister to chaperone. "We married when I was seventeen; we had a baby when I was eighteen, nineteen, and twenty four. 'That's all,' Archie said, 'no more children.' " Olamae and Archie bought land on Estee Avenue. In order to buy the property, Archie and Olamae picked and dried 14 acres of prunes at $150 an acre. Their first dwelling was a two-car garage with an outhouse; eventually they raised chickens, pigs, fruits, and vegetables. Archie became a tile setter and laid beautiful tile at the Native Sons Hall, the Oberon Bar, and the Lui Building on Main Street.

Ruth Raider met George von Uhlit at the Vichy Springs Pool in 1931. He was 19 years older than she, and her mother was not in favor of the marriage. They married anyway and bought their 40-acre farm in 1933 for $2,000 cash. Ruth spent her entire life on that land on Soscol Avenue just south of Trancas. She had four children, all born at home. She worked as a substitute teacher in the 1940s, although her husband disapproved. In 1943, they built a dehydrator and dried prunes, 10 tons a day. The farm also grew apples, walnuts, pears, peaches, persimmons, almonds, and apricots. When food was rationed in town during World War II, they shared their tokens and stamps with others. In 1947 Ruth and her husband built a swimming pool where she taught children to swim, because her heroine was Gertrude Ederle, who swam the English Channel in 1939.

Immigrant communities co-existed in downtown Napa. Dave Cavagnaro's Brooklyn Hotel at Third and Soscol continued to be the gathering place for the Italian-American community. Dave tended bar, sang songs, and played his concertina. His family lived upstairs; they rented rooms to single men working on the railroad and sold bootleg liquor through the back door during Prohibition. In 1930 Cavagnaro organized the first Italian-Catholic Federation convention and parade, and for 46 years he organized the Fourth of July and Fair parades as well. Cavagnaro spent 12 weeks every year traveling with the circus. On April 18, 1935, he put on a dinner at the Brooklyn Hotel for 35 performers from the Tom Mix Circus and Wild West Show.

Jane Smith describes a Swiss immigrant who lived downtown with his wife in a brown shingled house that they rented for $8 a month:

> During Prohibition they stored whiskey and made wine together. The women cooked. They ate outside under the fig tree on summer nights. Fragrant minestrone soup. Tender ravioli and malfatti. Platters of juicy sweet red tomatoes served with olive oil, vinegar and fresh basil. Strong beans off the vines, sautéed in garlic. Homemade noodles in butter and parmesan. They played the accordion, sang and drank red wine. . . . There were floods in the neighborhood, too, because everyone lived on the river.

Vanishing Places: The Dream Bowl and Shipyard Acres

> The river rose and claimed the basements. Everyone had pumps in the cellars. It was expected. Flood years provided excitement.

The river flooded in 1940, but that disaster was eclipsed in 1941 when the Japanese bombed Pearl Harbor. Citizens of countries with whom America was at war were required to register at the local post office. In Napa, 165 people registered as "enemy aliens." The part of town west of Jefferson and south of Third Street was zoned "A-1," the most sensitive for national security. No one of Japanese, German, or Italian descent was allowed to be there, even if they were U.S. citizens. The restricted zone included the heavily Italian neighborhood in East Napa. The Western Defense Command ordered all Japanese people out of Napa, Marin, and Sonoma Counties into internment camps; 54 were ordered to leave Napa County, all but ten of whom were first generation immigrants.

Juzo Hamamoto, a Japanese rancher from the Carneros district, was arrested and jailed. Virginia Norton, whose family chicken farm bordered the Hamamoto farm on Old Sonoma Road, remembers her mother "told us that if Mr. Hamamoto came on our property, she would hit him with a tree hook." She recalls that her mother's angry talk against their Japanese neighbors during World War II "didn't make sense to me"; Virginia later became an activist in the peace movement of the 1970s.

Because so many American citizens were involved in war work in the 1940s, growers persuaded the American government to create a "guest worker" plan, known as the Bracero Program, in California. It lasted between 1942 and 1964, and many workers stayed and established families in Napa. The Comite Mexicano de Beneficencia, founded in 1936 by Lucio Perez, provided burial insurance to Mexican immigrants and began to host fundraisers that functioned as community events. Quonset huts surrounded by barbed wire in the area of Rector Dam just north of Napa served as housing for Bracero workers in the 1950s; during the war these huts housed German and Italian prisoners of war.

There was a housing shortage throughout World War II and Napans were asked to make living space available to workers arriving from across the nation to work at the expanding Mare Island Naval Shipyard and the Benicia Arsenal. In January of 1942, chamber of commerce premises were donated for the entertainment of American soldiers who were temporarily camped at the Napa fairgrounds. Peter Gasser, chamber president during the war years, frequently presented checks and other forms of assistance to the USO, American Red Cross, and other agencies supporting the war effort. Napa families were encouraged to "dial a sailor" and to host military personnel assigned to the area for home hospitality and meals.

NAPA

One fifth of the 25,000 workers at Mare Island lived in Napa County. The Napa-Vallejo Highway was repaved since it was considered part of the National Defense Highway System. Because the war construction was so close to the city of Napa, air raid rules and blackout procedures were developed. Basalt built its first barge for the Navy in July of 1940. After the country entered World War II a complete shipyard, with four dry-docks, was built on Basalt property to provide ship maintenance. In 1942 it launched two U.S. Navy tankers onto the Napa River called the USS *Crownblock* and USS *Whipstock*. Basalt received the U.S. Army-Navy E Award in recognition of an outstanding production record. After the war they converted to peacetime production, making steel pipes to transmit water, oil, and gas.

Food rationing began in 1943. Commercially packed fruits, vegetables, juices, and soups were all rationed, as was coffee, meat, cheese, shoes (three pairs per year), and pressure cookers (75 to the county). Women received books of ration stamps that could be traded. Bernadette Traves told reporter Marcia Dorgan, "There definitely was a shortage of these things, but we all learned to make do with what we had. The coupons were redeemed at the grocery stores, and I mean grocery stores. Not these big, giant supermarkets like we have today."

The few restaurants that stayed open had to submit their menus to the ration board to prove that they were within limits. During the war there were frequent dances at the fairgrounds; Dave Cavagnaro's son Ray ran the liquor concession, and his brother Bob remembers dancing to the Dorsey Brothers and Benny Goodman.

Madeline Ontis went to work at Mare Island in May 1942. Born on Main Street, she was interviewed by Nancy Baker for a collection of memoirs by women workers and recalls:

> Napa is all I've ever known. As I look back, I have no bad memories—there were bad times but I was taught it could be worse. . . . I worked swing shift and there's no place colder on earth than swing shift on Mare Island. We had a small crew, we were called a gang, and everybody was good to us. There were just a few of us to start. I was just a kid. I was skin and bones.
>
> The fellows would come in off the ship and they knew how gullible I was. They asked for a left-handed monkey wrench. Probably today they have left-handed monkey wrenches. With all seriousness, I would search and search and finally I would go ask one of the men in the shop, and they would say, "Tell them we don't have any left."

Vanishing Places: The Dream Bowl and Shipyard Acres

Former welder Margaret Almstrom recalls, "All the girls I went with wanted to be welders and I didn't. I wanted to drive a truck." A friend got her into welding with a small trick—she put her hand up behind Margaret's head—and Margaret heard, "All the welders and YOU [Margaret] come with the lady boss to be trained to weld." Margaret started at third class, while those in first class earned $10 an hour. She wore jeans at Mare Island and describes it as the only place women didn't have to wear a dress. She remembers with a smile how a male welder got angry with her and raised her helmet while she was welding; as a result, she couldn't see for a couple of days. Almstrom worked at Mare Island until World War II ended. She was offered a job welding lightweight material after the war but "I couldn't keep my spark down low." At the age of 80, she comments wistfully, "When I see a sign saying 'welder wanted,' I always wonder if I would be able to strike up a weld."

After being laid off, Almstrom became pregnant. She got a job at the City of Paris shop in Vallejo, but "didn't like selling things." Her friends told her to apply at the state hospital, but her mother warned her "I'll give you two weeks, and you'll be home." Margaret's first shift was a night shift, and she jokes that she needed a "strong back and a weak mind" for her position. People asked her, "Do you lock the real bad ones up in those towers?" She would reply, "Yeah, the real dirty mops and wash rags!" When she worked there they had only one nurse at the facility. Margaret states:

> Whoever was on the ward had to be ready for anything to happen; no training was provided to handle mental patients. We had to sew our own uniforms; they couldn't be purchased anywhere; I wore a white uniform fashioned into a one-piece dress and a nurse's hat. Finally, nylon was invented and we were allowed to buy uniforms.

The Works Projects Administration, a program of the New Deal, described the state hospital in 1941 as "a jumble of gingerbread gables, turrets, and cupolas." In Dorothy Bryant's historical novel, *Confessions of Madam Psyche*, she describes a first view of The Castle:

> Marble window trim curved downwards to form faces, both human and animal, next to naked plumbing pipes added recently. These little carved faces—appearing the way fevered hallucinations might grow out of bumps on shadowy walls—were everywhere, most of them eroded into leprous, menacing expressions by many decades of weather. Other carved faces grinned from columns rising to and from the balcony. Below the balcony,

draped human figures stood in alcoves. . . . It [the smell] was as much a part of the building as its brick walls and maple floors—indeed it permeated walls and floors, especially floors. It was made up of many things, but its chief components were human waste, dry rot, and floor wax.

The women inmates would rise at 5 a.m., line up for breakfast, and then be given a "block" to clean with. This block was made of heavy wood, about two feet square, and was attached to a rough pole. It had an old blanket wrapped around it. She describes its use:

> In every ward, every morning, troops of patients pushed the blocks back and forth, up and down the long halls, polishing the dark rotten maple floors which, no matter how permeated with foul-smelling matter dropped over the past seventy years, always shone, slick and slippery. In some wards the block was called the major form of therapy; the first prescription by an attendant for restless, distracted patients was to "put her on the block."

Bryant, who interviewed official public liaison officer and unofficial hospital historian Ellen Brannick as well as former patients and attendants for her research, describes the hundreds of cats on the hospital grounds. One attendant said that the cats had been brought originally to keep rats out of the dairy, but an inmate "shook her head and said they were the descendants of pets brought from Napa and abandoned 'just like us.' "

There were eight doctors for 4,000 inmates, with visits that were "nothing but ceremonial." Although patients could earn passes allowing them to go to town, many never left the ward. They said the town of Napa was too far away to walk, or they lacked trolley fare, but the real reason was that patients, with their faded cotton sack dresses, heavy shoes, and lopsided hair cuts, felt conspicuous and judged in downtown Napa.

At the hospital, "three meals a day, for four thousand inmates, were cooked then transported underground on railcars by mules that, like mules in mines, never saw the light of day." A still was operating clandestinely in the castle cellars, and the alcohol was distributed free to the staff. The Fourth of July celebration was the highlight of the year as a marching band of male attendants and floats made by inmates traveled up the main drive. The mayor of Napa gave a speech from the balcony of the Castle, and there were fireworks. Participation was limited to working patients with passes, nearly 1,000 men and women. Visitors, staff, and their families made up another thousand attendees.

Vanishing Places: The Dream Bowl and Shipyard Acres

The hospital staff was supplemented during World War II by conscientious objectors. One of them explained, "I don't blame the attendants for not caring. The pay is terrible, they get no training, and they've each got seventy or eighty men or more. I'd like to organize them, lead a protest. But I can't, because they won't speak to me." Later, articles by these objectors led to reforms in the treatment of psychiatric inmates. Bryant describes a pile of wood on the main drive around the hog farm, which marked the graves of unclaimed and unnamed inmates. The state hospital later switched to cremation and used most of the wooden markers for firewood.

Next to the hospital was Napa's post-war government housing project, Shipyard Acres. Mildred Collins writes:

> The prolific farm and orchards of the Napa State Hospital were adjacent to the Acres. To the south—what is now Napa's industrial park—lay a wonderful marshland filled with flocks of singing blackbirds, both solid black and red-winged. Frogs took over the chorus on cool, breezy nights; nights when the stars and moon seemed close enough to reach up and touch.
>
> The tract was pretty much a self-contained village and a godsend for World War II vets and families who had endured transient lives along with less than desirable housing all during the war. The kitchen-dining areas had large pantries equipped with a stationary rinsing tub and space for a washing machine. We'd been lucky enough to find a used square-tubbed Maytag with an excellent ringer . . . a blessing compared to washboards. Detergent and instant starch had been unheard of yet.
>
> There was a grocery store that stocked the basics. And over on the west side of town, Stewart's Dairy sold glass gallon containers of unpasteurized milk with a thick topping of pure sweet cream. The store had lots of penny candies and a very tolerant staff. Without encumbering fences, kids were free to roam.

Another positive result of the war was the fact that most of the first generation of Napa Junior College teachers were World War II veterans. The college was part of Napa High School between 1944 and 1965. Bob Bernard was the assistant baseball coach as well as a teacher of history. In 1948 he and Paul Lathrop coached a baseball team that won a league championship for the first time in over 20 years. When Marie Ross interviewed him almost half a century later, she found that "Bob's phenomenal memory permitted him to name the entire team." Bob told Marie that "everything was new and fresh after the war and the college, really just beginning, was caught in a tide of great optimism." Bob Bernard wrote his own text in American History when the state required students to study government and he collaborated with the city manager of Napa on a booklet. Bob recalled the weekly lunches at faculty homes, "It wasn't fancy," he explained, "we just threw out bologna and bread."

Another early faculty member was Georgiana Lyons, who began teaching physical education in 1944. Her students played field hockey, basketball, badminton, tennis, and softball. Physical education classes became co-ed in 1948, and she added classes in archery and fencing. Lyons also competed in fencing in a Bay Area league.

Among the first students was Corky Scherette, who attended the college from 1949 to 1951, living in the student housing provided for football players. He later established the Glen Dubose Golf Tournament to honor "Pop" Dubose, who had been Corky's teacher and coach. One of the first graduates was Dorothee Farber-Braid. Her father fled Nazi Germany in 1938 to become the first pediatrician in Napa. She recalled in an interview with Tandy Miller that the "level of teaching was high and demanding" at the college.

Napa educator Dee T. Davis created what may have been the first Napa history course taught at the junior college. Davis was fascinated with the history of the indigenous peoples of Napa and took students from the Oak Grove School on field trips to the now vanished town of Monticello, where they collected artifacts such as arrows, pipes, charm stones, shells, and prayer stones. When Davis retired in 1948, the *Napa High Annual* was dedicated to him: "It is to this man who has helped to preserve the memory of the Indians of Napa County that we dedicate this book." Nancy Brennan explains that Davis had hoped his collection of artifacts might be displayed at Napa Junior College; instead, his son donated the 1,600 relics to the Museum of Anthropology at Berkeley.

The Napa Historical Society was also founded in 1948. Eighteen men and women met at the Plaza Hotel to elect officers. Eventually Ruth Bickford Northrop became its president. Her husband died of pneumonia, due to a shortage of antibiotics, during World War II. She returned to Napa with her two children, moved back into the family home with her mother, and found a job at the city health department. In 1930 there had been only 6,437 people living in Napa; by 1950, that figure jumped to over 13,000.

This nineteenth-century photograph depicts basket-making very typical of the Napa area. (Courtesy of California History Section, California State Library.)

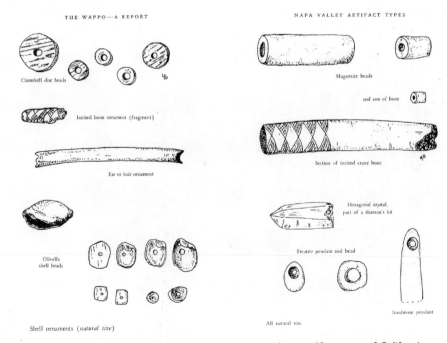

These are the tools used by the Mey'ankmah to pound nuts. (Courtesy of California History Section, California State Library.)

John Marshall's assistant, Sam Pitt, served as his *"spirit guide"* to discover gold. (Courtesy of California History Section, California State Library.)

This nineteenth-century engraving depicts indigenous people canoeing across the San Francisco bay.(Courtesy of California History Section, California State Library.)

General Mariano Vallejo was a wealthy Mexican soldier who settled on the Sonoma/Napa frontier. (Courtesy of California History Section, California State Library.)

Attacking bears on horseback was a common form of entertainment for the Californios. (Courtesy of California History Section, California State Library.)

Cayetano Juarez, pictured at left with his son, gave his Tulocay Rancho to Napa for use as a cemetery in 1859. Below, an indigenous woman living in Warm Springs; many native Napans were forcibly removed to Sonoma County in 1850. (Courtesy of California History Section, California State Library.)

J. J. SWEET,
Dealer in FRUITS, NUTS, CONFECTIONERY
Toys and Fancy Goods.
Main Street, Opp. Napa Bank,   NAPA CITY, CAL.

At right, Napa's abundant fruit and nut trees provided the ingredients for the products sold in this downtown store, J.J. sweet, in the early l900s. Below, the actual models used by James Earle Fraser for his famous sculpture "The End of the Trail," stand in front of the sculpture at the Pan-Pacific Exposition in 1915. (Courtesy of California History Section, California State Library.)

Napa City from the courthouse looking west, 1866.

The Napa Courthouse was built in 1856.

Included in this 1899 Sawyer Tannery photo are: Ah Chong, Mr. and Chas Philips, and Joe Azetti (first row); Robert Thompson, Jack Wilson, and Ike Wilson (second row); Louie Cassayre Ezette and George Wilson (third row); August Manasse, George Thompson, B. Imperialle, and Louis Banchero (fourth row).

The St Helena *steamer, a sternwheeler, had 25 staterooms. It began its run in 1902.*

The Trancas, Napa, Cal.

Horses drinking at Trancas, now the most crowded street in town.

Produce was transported by mule teams from the valley into the city of Napa.

The Napa Asylum aimed to be a model for the nation in the treatment of madness.

Napa Glove Company opened in 1876 on Soscol Avenue.

The Palace Hotel became the biggest lodging in the city with the "palace stables" having room for 45 horses. There were separate waiting rooms for men and women waiting for their horses to be brought around.

Napa Woolen Mill, opened in 1885, produced blankets for the Army, Navy, and the Alaska Territory.

This Chinese man is still wearing his queue (a braid to indicate adulthood) but also has a picture of William Henry Taft, candidate for President in 1909, pinned to his shirt to indicate his political interests. (Courtesy of California History Section, California State Library.)

In 1880, one out of every 13 people in Napa was Chinese.

The Napa Joss House was both a spiritual and a community center.

The Sam Key Laundry building at 58 North Main is the only surviving evidence of the Chinese presence in Napa (It is now a wine store.)

Saloons and butcher shops were vital businesses early on because of the importance of cattle ranching and the legacy of the gold miners. Pictured here is the Fagenbeyer Saloon with Bob West, gunsmith; Oscar Fagenbeyer, owner; Evens Meat Shop butchers Will O'Connell and Ed Kathan; and bookkeeper Mark Pearch.

Charlie Levinson and Abe Strauss opened Levinson and Strauss and then separated into two stores, Levinson's Clothing Store and Abe Strauss' Men's Wear.

When the College Equal Suffrage League offered a prize of $50 for a poster, Bertha Boye won with this entry in 1911.

Suffrage leaders, 1896. Lucy Anthony, Dr Anna Shaw, Susan B. Anthony, Ellen Sargent, Mary Hayes (first row); Ida Husted Harper, Selina Solomons, Carrie Chapman Catt, Ann Bidwell (second row).

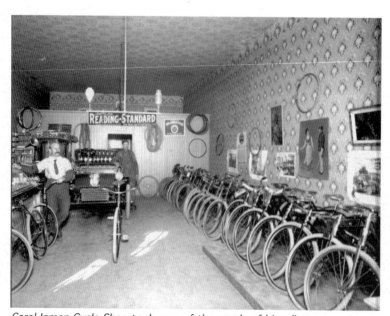

Carol Inman Cycle Shop took care of the needs of bicyclists.

Reading room of the Goodman Library, the first library in Napa, was founded in 1901 (Courtesy of California History Section, California State Library.)

Bryant's Tea Room and Candy Store was the place to go downtown. (Courtesy of California History Section, California State Library.)

Elmer and Robert Bickford on Clark Hill behind Connelly Ranch. The view is of Browns Valley looking northwest in the spring of 1911.

Elmer Bickford's wife Ada, his daughter Ruth, son Robert, and their dog Pepper on Redwood Creek, c.1910.

Every year the Napa Fire Department put on a Fourth of July parade. In the carriage is Mrs. Harry Monte at age seven. Fourth from the right is Dave Cavagnaro.

Chief Charles Otterson (from 1906–1943) is on the left with Gow Ling, known as "Dupee," a callman, and Otterson's older brother George.

The 1911 Fourth of July Parade on Main Street between Second and First.

Cherries were an important part of Napa's agricultural production. Napa Chamber of Commerce took first prize at the California Cherry Carnival in Santa Clara, June 1914.

The Napa Hotel was built in 1851, burned down in 1884, and rebuilt without the turret, which was later added.

Napa Baths was an indoor pool and steam room located at the present site of Community Projects.

Virginia Tallman grew up in this house on Polk Street where she could watch the Fourth of July parades go by every year.

NAPA VALLEY
═══ROUTE═══

SAN FRANCISCO, NAPA AND CALISTOGA RAILWAY
ELECTRIC
IN CONNECTION WITH
MONTICELLO STEAMSHIP CO.

TIME TABLE
Subject to Change Without Notice
EFFECTIVE MAY 15, 1927

STAGE CONNECTIONS AND THROUGH
TICKETS SOLD TO ALL IMPORTANT NAPA
AND LAKE COUNTY SPRINGS and RESORTS.

OFFICES

MONTICELLO S. S. Co., North End Ferry Bldg ....Phone Sutter 371
PECK-JUDAH, 672 Market Street....................Phone Kearny 2751
VALLEJO WHARF..Phone 14
NAPA STATION ....Phone 19
ST. HELENA STATION ....Phone 48
CALISTOGA STATION.................................Phone 17-M
C. E. Brown, Vice-Pres. and Gen'l Manager, NAPA, CAL.

This map shows the route of the Napa Valley Electric Railroad. (Courtesy of California History Section, California State Library.)

VB & NVRR electric train at the depot in 1906.

Napa High School, founded in 1897, as it looked when it was first built.

The girls basketball team at Napa High in 1912.

Mildred Pearch on left and Ruth Bickford on right in 1921 on Madison Street. Ruth was born in the house behind the car.

Olamae Combellack to the right of her mother, pictured at Gardeners Auto Camp with siblings, in 1924.

An advertisment for Boman Dairy from the 1924 Napa High Napanee.

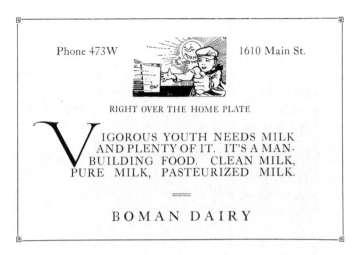

Phone 473W   1610 Main St.

RIGHT OVER THE HOME PLATE

Vigorous youth needs milk and plenty of it. It's a man-building food. Clean milk, pure milk, pasteurized milk.

BOMAN DAIRY

Have you a nice creepy book?
Yes. Are you a bookworm?

A postcard of Fuller Park, founded in 1905.

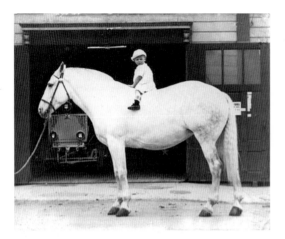

Rob Benson, on his horse "Fly," taking part in the Napa Firefighters Fourth of July Parade in 1906.

Members of the Unity Hose Company celebrating the installation of an electric fire alarm. They include, second from left, Charles Levinson, who sold menswear; tenth from the left, George Goodman Jr, founder of the library.

Young men leaving for World War I gathered in front of the Napa Courthouse and then marched to the depot to board the train on October 8, 1917.

Armistice Day Parade, 1918. In the front row are Donald Pond, Robert Bickford, Felton Watson, David Wright, and Elmer Bickford. The men are wearing masks because of the flu epidemic.

Magnavox inventors Peter Jenson (left) and Edwin Pridham. (Courtesy of California History Section, California State Library.)

The Third Street Bridge under construction in 1931 with the Palace Hotel in the right background and Noyes Lumber in the right foreground.

Downtown Napa in the 1930s. (Courtesy of California History Section, California State Library.)

Fox Theater was open from 1920 to the late 1940s on the northeast corner of First and Randolph.

Luis Vega, who came to Napa County in the 1940s as part of the Bracero Program, is pictured here with his wife Josefina Vega-Cuevas. His daughters Emma and Josefina moved to Napa City in 1989.

Olamae Combellack's mother Martine with her prune harvest crew and employer Mr. Mackenzie.

Flood waters rise east of Third Street in January 1940 as several onlookers pause to observe. *(Courtesy of Cathy Briles.)*

Soscol Avenue, now known as Auto Row, in 1947.

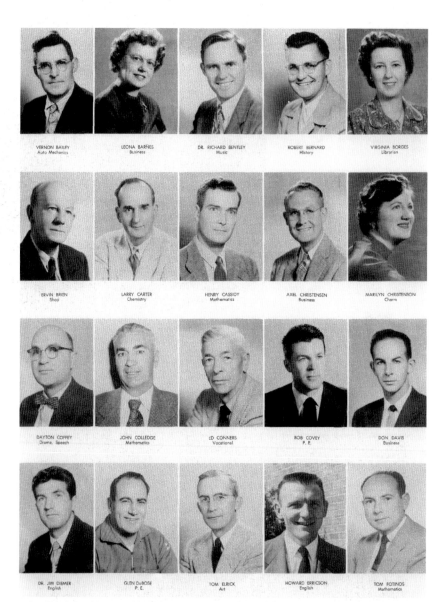

VERNON BAILEY
Auto Mechanics

LEONA BARNES
Business

DR. RICHARD BENTLEY
Music

ROBERT BERNARD
History

VIRGINIA BORGES
Librarian

ERVIN BRIEN
Shop

LARRY CARTER
Chemistry

HENRY CASSIDY
Mathematics

AXEL CHRISTENSEN
Business

MARILYN CHRISTENSON
Charm

DAYTON COFFEY
Drama, Speech

JOHN COLLEDGE
Mathematics

ED CONNERS
Vocational

BOB COVEY
P. E.

DON DAVIS
Business

DR. JIM DIEMER
English

GLEN DuBOSE
P. E.

TOM ELRICK
Art

HOWARD ERRICSON
English

TOM FOTINOS
Mathematics

The faculty of Napa College is pictured here, when it was still part of Napa High School.

Like his father Henry, David Wheatly spent his life farming prunes and still prefers them. Here Wheatley and Mr. Eisley of Sunsweet Growers converse at the Wheatley orchard in September 1951.

Theresa Tamburelli, inventor of the malfatti, with her sister Rosie Martini in the 1920s.

Napa State Hospital in 1931.

Margaret Almstrom was an orderly at the Napa State Hospital in the 1950s.

Margaret Almstrom was also a welder at Mare Island in the 1940s.

In the 1950s First Street was the center of everyone's lives.

*Carol Raahauge (right) in 1951
with best friends Hilde Dusen
and Connie MacLean (left),
taken at the county fair. Carol
grew up on Hagen Road Dairy.*

*Napa teenagers liked
to gather at the
Wright Spot on
Soscol Avenue.*

Pete Gasser's Dodge and Plymouth dealership featured a lubritorium.

A Napa City garbage truck in 1958.

A charter member of the Moose Club, Olamae Combellack pledges to bring "Mooseheart standards into homes and communities."

George and Mary Ellen Boyet were married at the First Methodist Church by Reverend Andrew Juvenal in 1963. Fellow Napa College teacher Hod Erricson was best man.

Virginia Tallman sells her Raggedy Ann Dolls at the County Fair in the 1960s.

Two of the first women teachers at Napa College: Dolores Fischer and Joyce Diemer, 1963 (courtesy of Community Relations, Napa Valley College).

FUTURE HOMEMAKERS: Front Row: Jan Smith,Dave Stinelli, Kevin Kiser, Mike Bosch, Wayne Miller. Second Row: Bill Adler, Steve Foster, ChrisFry, Jim Bondon, Tim Wolfe, Cort Sinnes.

FUTURE HOMEMAKERS: Top to Bottom: Diane McKenzie, Cathy Cole, Teddy Folsom, Nellie Solis, Kathy Mellow, Christy Hickey.

This section of the Napa High Yearbook for 1968 features "future homemakers," both male and female.

Brewsters was beloved for its ads in The Register, *which brought unique humor and wit into the life of the town.*

Ronald Reagan with Julian Weidler, owner of Rough Rider, during his 1970 visit.

Polly Wagenknecht, 4-H leader and community organizer, died at the age of 44 on New Years Day, 2000. Her obituary stated that she was survived by "all of Napa."

Napa citizens enjoyed a Browns Valley full of prune trees and thus voted in 1975 for a General Plan that would limit development.

Above, Napa Freeze gathers to march in front of Zeller's in Third Street as tireless organizer Susan Levine orchestrates with a megaphone. Below are the women of the Freeze in 1984. From left to right: (Top row) unknown man, Barbara Stancil, Rachel Hall, Helen Moser, Jeannine Scott; (bottom row) Dorothy Wonder, Marty Fotinos, and Virginia Norton.

Above, a celebration of the twentieth anniversary of the Napa College Women's Re-entry Program in 1995. From left to right: (front row) Lisa Meneeley, Sudie Pollock, Virginia Norton, and Evie Trevethan; (back row) Michele Jones, Hope Lugo, Kit Hall, Ana Kolwakowski, Wendy Ramsey, Judy Nelson, Joy Lancaster and Dana Hiney. Below, Napans protesting U.S. policy in Central America, early 1980s including Kathryn Winter and her daughter Joanna, far right.

"Women who made History in Napa" were honored at Napa College in 1983. From left (front row): Hope Lugo, former Head Start mother who became the director of Napa's anti-poverty agency; Serena Cochran, who designed and taught a class on survival as a single mother at Napa College; Elsie Crane, who fought successfully to "Keep Coombsville Green"; and Maryellen Boyet, who helped organize the National Women's Political Caucus in Napa.

Two drama teachers who helped organize adjuncts at Napa College and founded Sunseed Theater Company: Joel Mills and Terry Lamb, 1980.

Teachers Parker Hall and Janet Borba with their students at Silver Pony School in 1982.

Ruth von Uhlit was one of the last holdouts as a family farmer; she worked tirelessly to save open space.

The Napa Labor Temple, originally the Napa Steam Laundry, was where union members met and paid dues. By 1990 it was transformed into an office building. (Courtesy of Napa: An Architectural Walking Tour.*)*

Merrills, the last downtown drugstore, closed in the l980s. (Courtesy of Napa: An Architectual Walking Tour.*)*

Chef Clemente Cittoni in his kitchen at the Depot Restaurant in 2003.

Larry Friedman poses before the 1998 closing of beloved Napa institution, Brewsters.

Jason Guiducci with prune boxes, August 1981. The Guiducci family raised prunes since the turn of the century.

The 1986 Flood at the Cinedome Theater.

An anti–Gulf War protest, 1991, in front of Napa Post Office; holding a sign front and center is Reverend Owen Grams.

"Women who made History in Napa" Marlene Loseth and Carol Franco, union members who participated in the first and only strike of women clerks at Carithers, speak to Mary Ellen Boyet (left) c. 1983.

Headstart parents and children protesting the firing of teacher Fannie Chamberlain, one of the issues in the union organizing drive, c. 2002.

Krug workers protest from a roadside platform in January 2002. These workers were locked out of Charles Krug Winery for eight months. They are the last unionized production crew in the Napa wineries. From left, Hope Lugo and Betty Martin.

Chapter Eight

CIVIL RIGHTS AND SIDEWALK DAYS

People of every place in time deserve a history. Only local and regional history satisfies the need to remember the most intimate matters, the things of childhood . . . the goods, machines and tools with which they worked, and the groups in which they were raised, in which they matured, celebrated, had ambitions, retired, and resigned themselves to their fates . . . what they thought; how they felt; what they got angry, fought, and cursed about; what they prayed for; what drove them insane; and finally, how they died and were buried.

–Joseph Amato, *Rethinking Home*

In the 1950s and 1960s family life flourished in Napa, as in the rest of America. Unionized industries throughout the country provided good wages and the opportunity for workers to buy homes. Locally, the community college and its faculty brought a new liberal and intellectual spirit to the community. Some Napans remember the blooming of civil rights and the anti-war movement in their town during these decades, while others recall the simplicity of life in a small town encircled by orchards with drive-in restaurants, a skating rink, and two bowling alleys. Family businesses grew in Napa during this time; some survived into the present and others were forced to close with the invention and expansion of chain stores. Napa women joined clubs, made crafts, and worked outside the home in factories or in their own stores. Industry and agriculture were central to sustaining a small community town where everyone knew their neighbors, and many people married their high school sweethearts.

Margaret Almstrom, who had worked as an electrician's helper during World War II, raised her daughters Nancy and Peggy in a house on Janette Drive that she purchased for $8,000. Low housing and rental costs allowed many unique small businesses to exist; for example, Peggy worked at Mr Pennington's pet store on Pearl Street. She was allowed to take the ocelots and the honey bear home and dress them up in doll clothes. Women's lives were made easier by the existence of deliverymen: Colonial Bakery as well as Stornetta's Dairy provided home deliveries, and Nancy recalls that "the drivers would give us ice to eat."

Nancy remembers that Thursday night was "cruise night," when everyone went to the A&W on Silverado Trail and Third Street. She attended dances with live bands at the fairgrounds, and her friends bowled at Napa Bowl and Bel Aire, which were located at each end of town. The skating rink on Juarez Street sponsored competitions with prizes for the most graceful skaters. Napa High students gathered at either Kenny's Drive-In on Jefferson or The Wright Spot on Soscol. Nancy and her friends went to the KVON drive-in theatre on Foster Road, where she remembers seeing *Yellow Submarine*.

Many young women in Napa joined softball teams, where they developed a sense of camaraderie and achievement. Under the leadership of their beloved coach and manager Ernie Collicutt, the Napa Shamrocks reached national prominence and their pitcher, Carole Nelson, established an All-American record in 1955. Collicut, who headed the Bartender, Waiters and Waitresses Union, devoted many years to promoting girls softball, and his efforts resulted in the building of the Kiwanis Girls Softball Field on Coombs Street.

Cathy Mathews, daughter of Cecil Mathews, grew up on Monticello Road during the 1950s. The rural neighbors of the Mathews family worked at Mare Island, Kaiser Steel, Basalt, the state hospital, and the veteran's home. Cathy's mother was a butcher during World War II, first at Purity Market, then at Safeway. Cecil was a union man and Cathy remembers going with him to pay dues at the Napa Labor Temple. She recalls that up and down Main Street were multitudes of bars: "That was the social life for blue-collar people in town." A highlight of her parent's courtship was to park on Main Street on a Friday night and watch the drunks move from bar to bar. Liquor and tobacco were the norm, but "if there was violence in the family, it was something that nobody talked about."

Cathy attended Silverado Junior High and found it "horrible" because of the class distinctions between children of the business and professional class and the blue collar and poor kids. She found an escape in the store Napa Book, which was located on the corner of Pearl and Main Street. It was owned by Speed Herveau, who had been a baseball coach for the San Francisco Seals, and his wife, who had been a children's librarian in San Francisco. They moved to Napa in the 1940s and opened their store where, Cathy remembers, "you could get newspapers from all over the world." When Cathy's grandmother took her there, the owners "would let you look at anything, in later years, even *The Joy of Sex*." When the Herveaus died in the 1970s, so did the book store.

In the 1950s and 1960s most small towns had a Jewish-owned dry goods store, described by Stella Suberman in *The Jew Store* as a place "where farm hands, share croppers and factory hands could buy inexpensive clothes, piece goods, and linens." Opened in 1955 by Morris Nussbaum, Brewster's began as such a store, on the corner of Main and Pearl Streets. Nussbaum's daughter Rachel and husband Larry Friedman owned an Army-Navy store on First and Market Streets in San Francisco. In 1960 Rachel and Larry moved to Napa when Larry and his brother-in-law Harris Nussbaum became partners. Rachel cried all the way to Napa because "it was a good place for kids, but not a lot of things to do." She had to get acquainted through her involvement with the schools, the synagogue, and working in the store.

Rachel remembers Napa in those days as a "real country town where everyone was very friendly." When the store had an outdoor sale, shoppers lined up for blocks. Louis Martini would drive up in his Cadillac clad in overalls; Rachel explains that "wine snobbery hadn't arrived." Brewster's supplied work clothes, boots, bedding, cots, and almost anything else that vineyard workers needed to survive. The Brewster's ads were always a highlight of the *Napa Register*, costing $800–$900 for a full page containing zany caricatures of Rachel, Larry, and the crew. Larry and Rachel employed "an assortment of wonderful people" like Ralph Greico, who had worked at Mare Island, and was employed at Brewster's until he retired at 90.

Other long-time Napa businesses also opened up during this time. Nick Cervone began working at a tailor's shop in Italy at the age of six. In 1949, he immigrated to the United States with his father. When he saw the Golden Gate Bridge, it reminded him of the harbor at Naples, and the Napa vineyards reminded him of Italy. The Cervones opened their tailor shop on Second Street in Napa in 1955, where they sewed with opera music soaring out of the radio. Neff's Office Supplies, which now is across the street from Nick Cervone, was opened during this same period. Neff's was originally located next to Napa Creek and Frank Neff's daughter Linda remembers fishing from the second floor window.

Joe Bell had worked at Mare Island as a sheet metal worker until 1945. After the war he established Bell Products in an old wagon-wheel barn on First Street. He began remodeling storefronts in Napa, then installed heating and air conditioning. Although he originally had only three employees, he later hired apprentices who joined the Sheet Metal Workers Union.

Wash Mannering quit his job as a fabric worker at Cameron Shirt to open the Fitch Grocery Store, which he operated with his wife at the corner of Oak and Seymour. Mannering, a member of the Garment Workers Union, had also been secretary and president of the Napa Labor Council. He was a member of the State Grange, and he and his wife worked at the monthly pancake breakfast at the Grange Hall on Hagen Road.

Mary Anne Doud founded Family Drug. She was the daughter of Italian immigrants and grew up in San Francisco. As a child she played for hours with an old scale, pretending to fill pill boxes. She worked for a dentist from the age of 12, translating for his Italian patients on Saturdays. He encouraged her to become a dental hygienist. On the day she was going to begin dental hygiene school, she stayed on the street car and got off at the University of California Pharmacy College. She became one of only six women to graduate in her class. She wasn't old enough to be a pharmacist, so she worked for I. Magnin, where she developed an interest in cosmetics and perfume.

Doud's family used to visit Napa by ferry and electric train, so when a pharmacy on Brown Street was available, Mary purchased it and relocated in 1950. Two years later she opened a second store at the Food City shopping center and named it Family Drug. She had the largest perfume department of any store in Napa, with over 200 different scents. She hired three employees and worked as pharmacist. A second pharmacist, Thomas Gracia, was hired in 1976. Mary Doud became president of the Napa County Pharmaceutical Association and developed scholarships for the study of pharmacy. Her husband, Jess Doud, became the director of the Napa County Historical Society.

In 1947 Joe Vallerga opened a market. His family had already been operating a truck garden on the Napa River, providing the town with fresh vegetables. Vallerga's first store was on the corner of First and Juarez in what has since become the parking lot of JV Warehouse Liquor Store. In 1955 Joe Vallerga built a second market behind the first and hauled the first store across the river, and in 1960 a third store was opened at Redwood Plaza.

Also in the 1950s, Silvia and Oz Wilson bought the Silverado Meat Market, which shared space with Silverado Produce (owned by Dick and Ruby Eubanks) and Silverado Grocery (owned by Clarence Rath and Fred Milliman). Sylvia describes it as "a one-stop shop and personalized service designed to meet the needs of the Napa homemaker. Our customers were made of the Who's Who of the city as well as working-class people who wanted the best their money could buy." At the time Safeway and Purity Market were the only two chain grocery stores serving the city of Napa. Sylvia worked part-time as a clerk in the produce department along with Ruby. "When our son Monte got out of the Army, he worked in the shop with his dad. He learned everything he knows from Oz and later went to work as a butcher at Travis Air Force Base." Their daughter Marlene cleaned the meat cases on the weekend for spending money.

The Wilsons were able to buy a house on Alabama Street in Alta Heights. Business prospered until the late 1960s and 1970s, when national grocery chains were able to offer a greater variety of services and better prices. "We just couldn't compete with what the chains could offer Napa shoppers and we were just about to go under when we sold out. Oz didn't want to sell the business, but there just didn't seem to be anything else we could do. We got what we could out of it and he went to work for Lucky's."

Some Napa women like Sylvia Wilson, Rachel Friedman, and Mary Anne Doud worked in business; others joined clubs. One of the most well-known was the Junior Women's New Century Club. *Napa Register*'s Kevin Courtney wrote:

> A half century ago when they were young, their social lives lit up the society pages of the *Napa Register*. Their fashion and high-spirited variety shows, teas and dances were reported in lavish detail as if the Queen of England herself were in attendance. They were members of the Junior Women's New Century Club, the closest thing to socialites that this small town could muster. "Junior Century Club to See Movie Tonight," read one headline in 1947. "Spring Styles Are Shown by Junior Century Club," read another. These ladies are now the Napa Women's Club, a dwindling group of septuagenarians, octogenarians and nonagenarians. The youngest of their 33 members is 72.
>
> Wilma Ward, 79, joined Junior Women when she was in her 20s, more than a half century ago. That's what Napa's younger set did in those days, she said. The 1940s and '50s were a robust time for women's social clubs, said Ward, who remembers putting on musicals at Napa High School and attending club dances.

Meanwhile, Olamae and Archie Combellack became leaders of the Napa Moose Lodge. The women produced a Moose Lodge Prune Recipe book and participated in decades of installation dinners. Another very important organization for women was the Order of The Eastern Star, affiliated with the Masons. Rita Bordwell was a member of the Keystone Chapter of this group, as well as secretary of the Napa Labor Temple for a decade, fire department historian, and life-long member of the First United Methodist Church. Writes Nancy Brennan, "If there was a major effort required for anything in Napa, it was likely someone would suggest 'asking Rita' for help and most likely received it."

Other native Napans, like Carol Raahauge, stayed active in the countryside. Carol, who had grown up at the Hagen Road Dairy, maintained a lifelong friendship with Hilde Dusen and Connie MacLean. As teenagers, they took the Greyhound bus to San Francisco to shop for the newest style of bathing suit to display at Vichy Springs

NAPA

Resort. After Carol married Bob Grant in 1954, she and her husband bought part of her family dairy. Hidden under the brambles, she discovered her mother's remaining three rose bushes. Carol restored the rose garden, developed it into over one thousand rose bushes, and named it The Secret Garden.

Virginia Tallman, who had once watched the Fourth of July parades from her house on Polk Street, was one of the first graduates of Napa High. She married her high school sweetheart, Topsy, who worked on the Fruehauf Ranch on Dry Creek Road cutting hay and pruning trees. He was elected constable for Napa County in 1966 and 1970. Virginia worked in a candy store on Second and Main, cooked her first turkey at the Oberon, and was the first salad maker at the original Red Hen Cantina Restaurant in the 1940s. Later she operated a dressmaking business from home, eventually specializing in Raggedy Ann dolls. She made as many as 300 dolls a year and sold them annually at the fair. The dolls were red-headed, like her husband Topsy. In an interview with the *Register*'s Lynn Penny, Tallman explained that she would stuff the dolls with old nylons and pantyhose provided by friends and relatives. As Penny described it, "Mrs. Lamar (Virginia) Tallman likes sewing, the theories of Henry Ford, and children."

The 1950s also brought an increase in immigration, when the Brambila family arrived in Napa from Mexico. Maria Brambila writes:

> In the beginning, I felt isolated and homesick. We were making ends meet to support the family, but it was difficult because of the different way of life we had to get acquainted. We made the best of it as well as we could, and the most satisfying of this new life was seeing our young sons going to school and adapting to the new chapter in their lives in a positive manner.
>
> We were in the seasonal cycles of agriculture, where I would take my three sons when they reached the age of nine years, and bring them with me to harvest prunes, walnuts, and grapes. Since I didn't have childcare, I would take my young daughters with me to care for them. My husband eventually acquired a position at Beaulieu Vineyards Winery, working as a maintenance worker and being the lead person for operating the machines during the harvest period. He worked at B.V. for 45 years. He was provided a home in Rutherford by the winery for us to live. We were fortunate to qualify to purchase a home in Napa. A little after we relocated to Napa, I began working at the garment factory Rough Rider, and then it was bought out by the Koret Company. I worked at this company for almost 10 years, until the Koret Company went out of business.

Civil Rights and Sidewalk Days

Her son Hector went on to work in the Educational Opportunity Program at Napa College, conducting outreach to Latino students.

Aurelio Hurtado came to St. Helena in 1955, to join his brother Elias, who had come as a bracero to work in the vineyards. Aurelio began working at Charles Krug, first in the fields and later in the bottling plant, where he met and married Rogelia Martin. He helped to organize his fellow workers, making Krug the first winery to sign a contract with the United Food and Commercial Workers Union.

Basalt remained a major local employer. In 1955 Kaiser Steel purchased the Basalt plant site, and expanded and upgraded it. A large assembly bay was added to the plate shop in 1956, and two years later a second finishing line was added to the pipe mill. The upgrade gave Kaiser Steel the largest production capacity for such pipe in the United States. Many workers began their careers with Basalt and retired from Kaiser, never working for any other employer. Ralph Edward McConnell, for example, was hired by Kaiser Steel after World War II and continued to work for the company as safety engineer through its construction of the Transamerica Pyramid in San Francisco in 1970.

Patty Langer's father C.R. was a boilermaker at Kaiser Steel. In 1959 he bought the house on Wilson Street where Patty still lives with her daughter. Patty recalls walking with her mother to Safeway, which was then on Second Street, and to Darr's "five and dime store." She remembers going to Woolworth's lunch counter, where they would order hot fudge sundaes and banana splits. Her happiest memories are of "Sidewalk Days" once a year, when she and her mother would go shopping. All of Napa closed down on Sundays and her mother, Esther Langer, said "you could roll the street up, it was so quiet." Esther sewed all her own clothes because the local department stores were too expensive. Every year they went to the Napa County Fairgrounds and "looked at every chick and every rabbit." Esther Langer won first place for her Voodoo Lilly two years in a row.

Patty Langer remembers what it was like when there was no freeway, and Highway 29, which runs through town, was just a stop sign. The area, now home to the "Premium Outlets," once held Purity Market, where she and her family could walk across the road to shop. Everything north of downtown was still ranches and open fields. Although the Langers, like most Napans, opposed increased development, they did not know how to protest the changes that were happening to the town. Patty explains that they had "no idea" how to go to city planning meetings.

June Stephenson, teacher and author, writes:

> I remember coming to Napa in 1953 with one daughter only a year old and the other three weeks old. There were 25,000 people in Napa and only one

high school. In 1954, Ridgeview Junior High opened, where I had my first full-time teaching job. In 1958, Redwood opened where I was also a teacher. Napa was the kind of town where you could go downtown on a Saturday morning and see many people you knew.

Except for Woolworth's I don't remember any chain stores in the 50's or very much into the 60's. I remember when K-Mart came on Lincoln Avenue there was fear from local merchants. We shopped for clothes at a store called Albert's on First Street. When I started at Ridgeview I cleared $30 a month after paying for babysitting, but that was $30 I wouldn't have if I had stayed home, and $30 a month made a big difference.

George Boyet came to Napa to teach at the community college in 1958. He met and married Mary Ellen Florea, a French teacher at Napa High, when the high school was part of the college campus. They attended church at First Methodist, where their minister, Andrew Juvenal, was a disciple of Gandhi. George Boyet describes Napa as a "6 p.m. town," meaning that people of color were harassed after dark and African-American employees at Napa State Hospital like Dr. Davis and Dr. Handy had to live on the grounds or in Vallejo.

Reverend Juvenal was appalled by the housing segregation he witnessed and in 1960 he created an Ecumenical Race Relations Committee. He requested that the congregation sign a pledge to buy and sell to anyone, regardless of race, and many people left his church in protest. In the summer of 1963 Juvenal's house was firebombed. The arsonist left crosses and Ku Klux Klan literature. To show support for Andrew Juvenal, George and Mary Ellen Boyet were married at his church.

George Boyet describes Napa College in the early days: "All of us participated in the life of the town." College founders Harry McPherson and Jessamyn West were liberals with a wide range of international friends with whom the faculty mingled. Many people who began teaching at the college moved on to other worthy projects, like Craig Walker, Director of Community Action, or Bob Frickman, founder of Napa County Legal Assistance Agency. Mary Ellen went on to become active in the teacher's union, while George Boyet chaired the Napa County McCarthy for President Campaign in 1968.

In an interview, college teacher Joyce Shane Diemer laughed as she recalled the 1965 move of the college to its present campus:

It was a muddy, unpaved, disaster in the worst condition; it was awful! Other things changed too, besides the environment. On the old campus the faculty was united as a group, and when we moved, that unity was gone. Most of the male teachers wore slacks and a jacket with a tie . . . as for the ladies, we wore skirts or dresses with heels until the Seventies.

Ginny Simms moved to Napa in 1955 and was actively involved in the development of the college. She told interviewer Marie Ross, "I found the school to be much misunderstood in the community at that time—people did think of the school as a continuation of the twelfth grade." The site for the new campus was picked because it could be purchased inexpensively from the state. State Senator John Dunlap secured the grounds for the campus and helped create nearby Kennedy Park, named to honor the recently assassinated president.

One of the many beloved original Napa College teachers was Hod Erricson. Hod's daughter Louise recalled:

> It was a Sunday afternoon in spring of 1964 or '65, and my dad, along with Jim Diemer, President of the College, and Don Macky, the College architect, took a walk around the fields opposite the State Hospital. They talked about plans and hopes for the new College, and it was their dreams that resulted in the structure we now have.

Louise has vivid memories of being a "faculty brat" in an era when the entire faculty seemed like an extended family:

> I remember being old enough to go to the Uptown Theater on Third Street with my parents, and taking twenty minutes to find seats because they knew everyone else in the entire place, lodge seats and all. Visits to Food City Grocery Store, the library or Walkers Restaurant took hours, due to all the chatting. For the local intelligentsia, who created their own entertainments and amusements, it was much more than a beautiful place to live and raise their families.

Mary Wallis attended the college from 1961 to 1963. Interviewed in 1992, she remembered Hod Erricson as someone who encouraged her to think for herself. She also remembered her French teacher Simone Fontaine, "She was very tall, and thin, and always wore floral dresses. She had the classic French red cheeks and we really liked her because she would call the guys jerks in French when they were goofing off."

NAPA

Before Napa College moved to its current site, there was both an official school paper and three "underground papers." Controversy erupted over George Link, a journalism teacher hired around 1965. George Boyet explains that Link was "part of the counterculture; he encouraged the students to protest the Vietnam War, and to write letters to soldiers in Vietnam urging them to lay down their weapons." Joseph Amato noted about the times:

> The Vietnam War washed directly onto the town's shores. At the college itself, subjects that were once considered forbidden were shouted from podiums. Students repeatedly poked the local population in its righteous eye. Again and again they challenged the moral unity of locale and nation—and acted out the illicit.

The editor of the *Napa Register*, Ross Game, started a campaign to deny tenure to Link. The faculty committee split on whether to give him tenure, voting not to recommend either way. The Faculty Senate met for three days in an emergency session and finally endorsed Link. President George Clark reversed the decision and the board abolished the journalism department, claiming it was a budgetary decision. There would never be another tenured journalism instructor at Napa College.

Napa High School was deeply affected by the student movements of the late 1960s, and began publishing its own underground newspaper in the fall of 1965. One issue included an account of Joe Morehead's visit to Mississippi; a sonnet by Don Laughridge on the death of American soldiers in Vietnam; a review of *Mr. Tambourine Man*, the new Byrds album, by Paul Hein; and an essay called "The New Society" by Dan Woodworth.

Patty Langer remembers her special teachers at Napa High, Mrs. Murdock and Dr. Payne (whom she calls "a bit of a radical"). Her entire family was against the Vietnam War, including her dad who was an atheist and a liberal thinker. He told Patty, "If none of the kids join the army, the big 'ol boys couldn't have the war," and she observed that everyone in high school grew long hair overnight to protest it. Her strongest memory of her teen years was walking door-to-door campaigning for Robert Kennedy in the California Primary in June of 1968. She was devastated by his assassination on election night.

Local activists also published the *Napa Valley Voice*, which included: "Know Your Rights" information in English and Spanish; an interview with Carol Erickson, the Chairman of the Napa Race-Relations Committee; and an announcement of the

Civil Rights and Sidewalk Days

Vietnam Moratorium at Napa College, which featured speeches by history instructors Tom Malone and George Boyet. In 1969 Napa High students published *The Third Estate*, with an essay by Lee Halterman condemning censorship, and an article on Women's Liberation by Dennis Patterson. Patterson, who was expelled in 1970 from Napa High for his political activism, remembers that he and his friends learned about the youth movement from visits to Haight-Ashbury, listening to KMPX, and reading underground newspapers.

Michael Amen recalls that "In February 1969, I headed across the city of Napa to attend a concert . . . it seems more fitting to think of it as a pilgrimage." Amen had seen an advertisement in the *Register* for a concert for the Grateful Dead at the Dream Bowl. The Dream Bowl had been mostly closed in the 1950s and Amen's mother told him how it had thrived during World War II, when "couples were looking for some romantic way to spend their time because it could very well be their last time together." Amen writes, "When the Dead performed, I was totally captivated . . . I feel lucky that I got there at that particular nick in time." Joseph Amato describes the changes that swept through America in this period:

> Wearing long hair, dressed to insult and provoke, living communally, smoking marijuana, and hatching anti-war protests, students were undermining all that America stood for. At least, that's how it seemed to older citizens shocked by their first experience with a college community, especially one caught up in protest.

Jane Smith experienced these changes as she raised her children in downtown Napa:

> We moved there when the rent was low as a creative solution to inflation. The day the house and I took our rental vows, I strolled around the outside first and was won over by an ancient fig tree that grew in the cement courtyard. Ripening figs have that special home town fragrance. There were benches and tables under the tree where the Italian families of the past, now gone, held their ravioli and malfatti dinners.
>
> We were a houseful of adolescents, Aunt Fodie and me. Queens are rich but I am richer in memories of that time. There was so much rebellion and seething and chewing on the bones of Vietnam, the draft, the pill, long hair. The assimilation of those changes, for them and for me, required endless hours of dinnertime talk.

NAPA

The growth of the Latino immigrant community continued, due in large part to the creation of the Agricultural Preserve in 1968, which quickly transformed orchards into vineyards. The California Legislature passed the Williamson Act in 1965, allowing the county assessor to consider the income potential of agricultural activity as the basis for taxation. University of California researchers told landowners that they could reap maximum profit from grape growing. Gary Brady-Herndon describes the fierce battle over agricultural zoning: "The discourse raged bitterly, sometimes between long-time friends and family members." Although most people did not expect orchards to be replaced by vineyards, this was the eventual result. As part of this transition, most growers stopped picking their own crops and increasingly relied on immigrant labor.

Meanwhile, in 1963 Aurelio Hurtado joined Louis Flores and others to organize a Napa chapter of the Mexican American Political Association (MAPA). Their goal was to register voters and educate the community. Hurtado remembers that "Lou Flores was the pillar" of what became a political organization called Low Income Families Together. Recent immigrants campaigned to open a local Office of Economic Opportunity, which quickly became a basis for community organizing. In 1950 Napa was home to less than 14,000 people, but by 1970 the population had jumped to 37,000.

Chapter Nine

"LIKE DAVID SLAYING GOLIATH"

Despite the miseducation they might have endured—or because of it—many people are hungry for real history.

—Michael Parenti, *History as Mystery*

For Napa, as for America, the 1970s and 1980s were a time of political awakenings and activism. The deindustrialization of America meant that Napa factories like Rough Rider and Basalt closed their doors, and department store clerks and housekeepers were forced to strike to protect their union jobs at Carithers Department Store and Silverado Country Club. The "slow growth" movement flourished, even as the orchards quietly began to disappear. The generation gap that had been developing in Napa, as well as throughout the country, became undeniable when Governor Ronald Reagan visited the Rough Rider factory in 1970 and hundreds of angry teenagers, calling themselves "Yippies," marched through downtown Napa. By 1972 a group of young women in Napa rented space on Third Street where they held "rap groups" to share their developing feminist consciousness. Within a decade the Nuclear Freeze movement also opened an office on Jefferson Street where it organized vigils, community dinners, and an "anti–Star Wars" Brigade in the Town and Country Fair.

One of the most important movements of this era was the community's resistance to sprawl and redevelopment. In the early 1970s the Napa Community Redevelopment Agency cheerfully reported:

> Not since its settlers decided that Napa should be more than a mere stopping place for riverboats or mainly a miners' refuge from the harsh winters of the Sierra foothills, have the sight and sound of new construction, public improvements, and general renovating proceeded at such a pace here. . . . Drab thoroughfares are being dressed up as tree-lined malls, topped by an exciting new plaza.

Nevertheless, the value of redevelopment was hotly contested, and many longtime Napans were reluctant to see their hometown so radically changed. Jane Smith reported:

> The city is getting a new city. The Migliavacca Building, a landmark of dove grey stone at First and Brown Streets, soon will crumple under the wrecking hammer. A modern department store in the urban renewal area will take its place. Century old trees, which gave the corner of Second and Seminary Streets its cool and shady aspect, have been destroyed for construction. The city is changing as never before . . . as fields and meadows fill up with new building, parking lots, stores, and apartments. Will the new city be as unique as the old, as beautiful and shady and comfortable? In fifty or a hundred years, will today's structures have been as graceful and enduring as the homes built in the 1800's?

Even the business community questioned the wisdom of redevelopment. Rachel Friedman, co-owner of Brewster's, recalls how a group of Main Street merchants formed Citizens Against the Destruction of Napa, using Brewster's as meeting place. She remembers that her husband Larry opposed the construction of a Clock Tower and took his fight all the way to the California Supreme Court, where they lost. She explains:

> Without Larry's efforts, the whole block on Main Street would have been wiped out, including the Opera House. Larry was a real political firebrand during that period of Napa history. Many of us urged him to run for mayor and I think he could have succeeded.

Former City Planner Mike Joell moved to Napa in 1968 at a time when redevelopment was in its infancy, there weren't any environmental issues in play, and the Agricultural Preserve had just been adopted. He recalls that although the county supervisors were all Republicans, their passage of the Ag Preserve bill led local farmers to denounce them as communists. Joell had previously been a planner in San Diego and Santa Rosa, where he witnessed the harmful effect of redevelopment. He recalls the destruction of historic buildings because they wanted to move in a modern direction and notes that every attempt to do so was met with opposition from the community.

Co-Op Extension Adviser John Wagenknecht cites Napa as an "example of the way community action can work" because citizens prevented sprawl and preserved open space for over a decade. He recalls that the organization included both blue-collar workers and professionals who worked at the state hospital. Headed by Harold Kelly and Barbara Corotto, they organized a group called Neighbor, which

"Like David Slaying Goliath"

Wagenknecht says "stormed City Hall." As a result, in the 1973 election, there was a referendum on development. The mandate of the voters was to maintain the size of the city as much as possible and to keep downtown as the center of the shopping district. In 1975 the General Plan echoed their concerns by planning only minimal population development for the year 2000.

One of the most committed activists was Rosemary Gill. She, her husband, and their six children founded a local chapter of the Christian Family Movement. In the early 1970s Gill was encouraged to apply for the Planning Commission, and continued to help others with their political campaigns. Longtime friend Ginny Simms told *Register* reporter Roseann Keegan:

> Rosemary understood the written word and how to simplify it, how to clarify it. She also would be personally energetic in the campaign. If she believed in you, you had someone who would make all kinds of efforts for you. I would say she knew more people in the community than anyone else I knew.

Meanwhile, Mike Joell joined other activists to save land for parks. In 1974 developers bought the 112-acre property, now known as Westwood Hills Park, in order to build 400 units of housing there. The planning commission offered them only 136 units, so they pulled out of the deal. Joell, Muriel Fagiani, and Barbara Corotto hiked up onto those hills overlooking the city, imagining its potential as a park. Mike Joell realized the redevelopment department would soon have $12 million available, so he and Corotto made a list of possible parklands. As a result, the city bought Westwood Hills Park for $150,000, as well as the property of Dr. Alston for $167,000.

Mike Joell founded the Napa Chapter of the Sierra Club in 1976 and met his wife Eva on a Sierra Club hike. At one of their regular potlucks, Joell told the members that there was a new park in need of trails and benches. Joell spent "at least a thousand hours per year on the park." As historian Richard Rice noted, these same issues were debated throughout California:

> Although most local governments remained firmly in the grasp of development interest, slow growth movements captured some city governments as early as 1970. . . . California's environmental organizations increasingly acted as adversaries to business and government. A few paid professionals led a growing army of volunteers, often women, in projects that took on the intensity of crusades. They backed or opposed candidates

for office on the basis for their stance on environmental issues. The decades from the 1960's–1980's were a creative period in resource and environmental policy.

Elsie Crane was another important organizer against the destruction of the countryside. She had worked on the railroad, been a beautician, and organized apple pickers in Sonoma County. When she learned that the Lewis Dairy was going to be developed into expensive housing, she helped found Keep Coombsville Green. The organization was successful in keeping the east side of town an agricultural region.

Although the fight to save agriculture was largely victorious, the crops themselves changed dramatically. Co-op adviser John Wagenknecht remembers looking over Napa and seeing nothing but blooms covered in snow, trees that bore prunes in the spring. Wagenknecht says the switch to a monoculture wasn't a healthy choice, but farmers paid attention to the market and growing grapes was always more lucrative. In 1977 Napa native Louis Ezettie commented sadly in his weekly newspaper column, "Once one of the great prune growing areas in the state, Napa County had seen the industry give way to an almost complete turnover to grape growing." Sunsweet disposed of the packing and shipping departments on Jackson Street, and reduced its workforce from 100 to 25 people. Ezettie wrote, "Napa Valley grown prunes, in my estimation, surpassed the quality of the fruit grown in other parts of the state. Every year we kids earned enough money picking prunes at the Frank Bush Ranch near Little Trancas to pay for school clothes and school books."

James Guiducci describes the problems faced by his family ranch, purchased by great-grandfather Carlo Brignoli, who came to Napa from Northern Italy after the turn of the century:

> The fields were plowed by a late 1930's model tractor, which ran until 1987 when the last crop was harvested at my grandfather's ranch. In fact it was one of the last operable prune orchards in the valley that was still selling to Sunsweet. Each August until 1987, my family would converge on the farm to help pick prunes. My cousins, aunts, and uncles would visit from out of town to help. In the past ten years, my grandfather has had his drinking water well re-drilled three times in order to find freshwater deeper. No doubt the vast acres of the new surrounding vineyards have put intense pressure on the finite aquifer.

"Like David Slaying Goliath"

Meanwhile, the expanding grape economy provided jobs to an increasing number of immigrant families from Mexico. Lilia and Jose Navarro arrived in 1980 from Michoacan, and Jose was hired as a vineyard foreman. At their first apartment on Collier Boulevard, Lilia recalls that other Latino and Anglo families made them feel welcome. When Lilia's daughters were at Shearer School, she suggested forming a Ballet Folklorico to provide culture to the children. Eve Hernandez, then the bilingual teacher, encouraged her, and Navarro's dance troupe was founded.

While the slow-growth movement resonated with many locals, others were preoccupied with the escalating Vietnam War. When then-Governor Reagan visited the Rough Rider plant and spoke to 500 people at the Elks Club, 200 young people marched through downtown Napa to protest the war and Reagan's attacks on the anti-war movement. Although some Napans welcomed the governor, few realized that his policy of state hospital closures would soon eliminate jobs many local families depended upon.

When Nixon invaded Cambodia in May of 1970, students at Napa College and around the country were outraged. When protesters lit trash cans on fire, college president George Clark ordered a newspaper for every classroom and encouraged faculty to hold a teach-in to give the students an outlet for their anger. That evening 300 Napans, led by George Boyet and Reverend Owen Grams, marched from the parking lot of the recreation department to a rally at Fuller Park. In 1980 Kevin Courtney interviewed rally participants for The *Napa Register*. Reverend Owen Grams recalled that some congregants left Emmanuel Lutheran Church because, interestingly enough, they thought peace didn't have anything to do with Christianity.

The political energy of the anti-war movement created both a sense of possibility and of experimentation. By the early 1970s Napa College students were publishing their own newspaper called *The Extra Rag*, published "when we can . . . for who we can . . . any way we can." It included an advertisement asking for anyone who was interested in joining a guerilla theater group, a coffee house, or wanted to contribute by creating costumes or masks, or playing music.

In 1971 Helen Hunter ran an ad in the *Napa Register* to discover how many parents were interested in an alternative educational experience. Thus Vintage 2000 was founded, a school in which the children, parents, and teachers created their own curriculum. Lois and Jim Engle were chosen as teachers and moved to Napa to work with the families. In the yearbook, Lois wrote:

> I didn't go to a school like this, and I never got to mess around with all
> those art materials before, and make musical instruments, and learn to fold

six dozen different kinds of airplanes. They don't listen just with their ears, they listen with their skin and eyes and everything else. They learned from different grown ups, not just me, or Jim, or Don, or Helen, or whoever the teacher happened to be, but there were all the other people.

Demonstrating the philosophy of its parents, the yearbook contains a letter from Laura Merritt to Governor Reagan asking not to kill any more mountain lions, especially baby ones, and Frank Tibbens penned his own essay about building a raft and sailing down the Napa River. Co-teacher Jim Engle commented:

> Lois and I thought "cooperative school" was a fine title for what we had in mind: people cooperating, working together as social mates toward a relatively common end. We in fact wanted structure. We wanted the children to feel relaxed about competition (no grades, no progress reports to haunt them), to share their feelings, to feel the worth of what they like to do.

Other alternative schools were founded shortly after this one; among them was Silver Pony School, located behind Highway 121 next to the gas station. Parker Hall and Janet Borba created a homelike atmosphere where children ranging from two to ten years old created theater pieces on the stage, made art projects and their own books, and where parents held monthly dinners and watched their children perform. Joel Mills of the Sunseed Theater Collective did shows with the children at Silver Pony. Like Joel, Sunseed co-founders John Marsh, Jan Molen, and Terry Lamb taught at Napa College. Marsh explains the theater group's philosophy:

> Playing in a theater meant you were playing to the wrong audience. We did not much care for separating the play from the audience, but commingled with them, doing shows in all available spaces: chicken coops, bookstores, tract homes, lawns, trailers, living rooms. When we *did* perform in a theater, we would perform in the lobby or in the chairs, never settling for "on stage." The idea was to break down the conventions of theater and the standard audience/performer relationship. Sunseed roots go back to an earlier time at Berkeley where most of us were students involved in Theater for Peace.

Schools like Vintage 2000 and Silver Pony created a climate in Napa in which some parents began to expect and then create alternatives within the public schools.

"Like David Slaying Goliath"

Teacher Lois Engle went on to develop a slide show about sexism in children's nursery rhymes and became part of the planning committee to develop women's studies courses at Napa College. John Marsh and Terry Lamb wrote a report for the Napa College Board about the status of part-time teachers, which was the impetus for a lawsuit by the California Teachers Association on their behalf. Lamb recalls:

> We had surveyed teachers of all kinds at the college to get a sense of what they did in their jobs and how many hours per week they worked. I remember that full-timers averaged 48 hours per week, and all teachers, including part-timers, reported doing roughly two hours outside of class for every hour in class. Some part-timers were working 25–30 hours per week and were getting substantially less than half-time pay, and no benefits. At that time almost 80 percent of the faculty were part-timers, and the hiring of full-timers with tenure had nearly ceased. When we heard about groups of part-timers at several other colleges, we joined with them to form the California Association of Part-time Instructors, which had a few glorious years in the mid-'70s.

The part-time teachers' lawsuit was settled in 1983, when many of the plaintiffs exchanged the back pay they were owed for full-time status as teachers at the college. Meanwhile, at Napa High school, change was also in the air. June Stephenson remembers:

> In the 1970s I sued the school district for discrimination for not promoting women into administrative positions, while promoting less qualified men. My particular suit dealt with a position for junior high principal at Redwood High School. The clincher for the discrimination case was a letter that the president of the board had sent me when my interview was over for that position. It said something about though I looked pretty as a woman, how would I as a woman be able to tell men what to do? The school settled out of court for the difference between what I would have been paid as a principal and what I made as a dean.

Stephenson found a book called *A Short History of Women*, published in 1928, in a used bookstore and bought it for 35¢. The ideas it generated were worth much more:

> I hadn't known there was a women's history. I had asked the principal at Napa High if I could develop such a course. The social studies department at Napa

High didn't want a course in women's history, but Tom Fotinos agreed that Napa High needed a course like that. He saved the course. Students said they had learned more about history than any history course they'd taken.

The social studies faculty voted it down again and stated women had too much power as it was. When Stephenson met with the teachers, they took a vote and wrote a letter to the principal in support of her efforts. She recalls that by the end of the day the social studies department would indeed include women's history in their department. Stephenson resigned after four years to write her own book, *Women's Roots*, which is still in print today. Women's history was again removed from the curriculum at Napa High and was only offered at Hill and Valley, a school program for pregnant teenagers created by Sudie Pollack. In an interview with Elizabeth Sagehorn, Sudie recalled:

> In the summer of 1963, my best friend at Napa High got pregnant and was kicked out of school. She wasn't allowed to be around the rest of us because, she was told, she had "carnal knowledge." She didn't get her diploma. She got married and lived a life of quiet desperation for many years. I saw what happened to her and didn't want that to ever happen to another girl.
>
> It was very apparent to me that we needed to increase the self-esteem of these girls. I used the whole month of March, which is Women's History Month, to acquaint my students with strong women. They were always so amazed to hear about Sacagawea and Rosa Parks. Watching my students over the years go through childbirth, which is a very difficult thing, raising children alone, dealing with difficult family situations, boys and men who sometimes walked away, made a raging feminist out of me.

Sudie Pollock developed Women's History Week celebrations in the public schools, which were held throughout the 1980s when there was a strong feminist movement in Napa. She also worked to open a Planned Parenthood office in Napa in 1978. Just before her retirement, she got back in touch with her best friend and found that her friend's mother "used to send her all the clippings about my school. It really touched her that I was able to provide a much better situation for other pregnant girls."

Many young Napa women experienced discrimination and a sense of hopelessness after high school. After graduating, Pam Brooks took a job at Silverado Country Club and describes meeting her fellow employees:

"Like David Slaying Goliath"

Seeing Eva nearly broke my heart. She was pushing sixty and had worked at the "club" for 20 years. She could not stand straight, her hands were gnarled and red, her eyes were lifeless. The only one of the group who was not motionless was 28-year-old Nancy; she was addicted to amphetamines. On and on they were introduced, each with her own story of defeat, futility—hopelessness. I wondered what I had gotten myself into.

Brooks wrote that her pure stubbornness was the only thing to get her through the first grueling week When she opened her first pay envelope and found that she had earned $92.40 for 56 hours of work, she thought it must be a mistake. She asked her boss about overtime pay:

"No such animal here," he replied curtly. "If you don't like it, plenty of others waitin' to take your place. However, I'm satisfied with your work, even gonna give you a raise if you decide to stay—nickel an hour. Customers are pleased too. Even gonna add some more "young skirts" to the staff" he said as he exited his office, leaving me sitting there in disbelief. His hiring of Christie, Paula and Candy the following week would soon prove to be one of the most expensive decisions of his career.

During breaks the workers began to discuss the fact that wealthy guests paid the same amount for one night's stay as they earned in a week. They were also concerned about the chemical concentrations far above the recommended labels, the absence of benefits, and how absurd it was to have to wear short, tight dresses required for work. They began a series of secret meetings with organizer Bill Richerson of Service Employees International Union (SEIU) Local 18. Brooks remembers that it was more difficult than first anticipated to convince co-workers of the benefits of union protection when they worried about "who else would hire an aging, uneducated, unskilled woman?" They also had to persuade waitresses and bartenders to join, but the employees eventually voted 48 to 2 for the union. Brooks wrote:

I was surprised how much this victory meant to me. We won a forty-hour week, time and a half for overtime and retroactive pay. The day the retroactive paychecks were passed out, Eva openly wept. Her check amounted to several thousand dollars.

NAPA

Thus did feminism rush into the lives of the women in Napa in the 1970s, just as it did in small towns across America. In 1972 a group of young women rented a downtown storefront at 1783 Third Street, named it the Napa Women's Center, and held regular meetings to address the inequities in women's lives. The group, which included Ana Kowalkowski, Jan Svoboda, Kit Hall, and Lois Engle, studied the epidemic of violence against women and developed local resources to address it. They schooled themselves about the missing gaps in their own education and advocated for a women's studies program at Napa College.

The Women's Center entered the mainstream of Napa when Lois Engle wrote an article for the Kiwanis Club's Ladies Night about feminism and child-rearing, as when Jay Goetting and Jane Myers invited speakers about feminism to a radio program on KVON. Members of the Napa Women's Center created both the Women's Re-entry Program and the Child Care Center at Napa College. Housewife Carol Raahauge Grant was inspired to return to college, where she received her M.A. in Sociology and became one of the first women's studies teachers at Napa College, teaching courses on marriage and family. Serena Cochran taught the first class on the single parent. One of the most popular courses, taught by Coordinator Evie Trevethan, was Assertiveness Training. A group of young students and teachers initiated a volunteer hotline for victims of domestic violence.

Mary Ellen Boyet and friends organized a vibrant chapter of the National Women's Political Caucus, which helped elect women to local and state office—and it paid dividends. Locally, Dorothy Searcy became one of the first women on the city council and Ginny Sims the first woman on the board of supervisors. In 1981 a petition campaign to the board of supervisors, and years of collecting signatures at shopping centers, resulted in the opening of a home for battered women and their children.

One of the key tenets of feminism was that women should be economically self-sufficient. Apprenticeships in blue-collar jobs offered new opportunities, and many Napa women applied for and received this training. One of them was Nancy Almstrom, who had worked as a bartender and waitress after high school. In 1977 she applied for a position with the City of Napa for an electrician's helper. With the "I-can-do-anything" attitude, she took the job, which she held for eight years. She and a female co-worker found no women's facilities in the Napa Corporation Yard and were sometimes disrespected by male co-workers. Nevertheless, they blazed a trail for women to follow. In 1983, while pulling cable in front of Lyon's Restaurant, Nancy sustained a work injury and could no longer perform her job. She had to take a clerical position, but was never happy working in an office as she "felt like an animal who wanted to be outside."

"Like David Slaying Goliath"

International politics mobilized many Napans with the 1980 election of Ronald Reagan as president. Peace activist Randall Forsberg's call to "freeze and reverse the nuclear arms race" initiated the Nuclear Freeze Weapons Campaign, a grassroots based confederation of groups across the country. Led in Napa by a group of women that included Rosemary Gill, Barbara Stancil, and Lynn Baker, the Freeze campaigned in 1982 for a congressional ballot initiative. Dorothy Raymond recalls:

> I opened the Napa Freeze office in my living room for the first six months in 1982. In August, my then high-school-age son Charley and his friend Steve Capovilla made a long banner reading "No More Hiroshimas," and very early one morning they climbed the green bridge near where Jefferson dead-ends into the shopping center to hang that banner. He recalls the *Napa Register* printing a picture of it—and a day or two later, when starting off on one of those inimitable trips with Al Lilleberg, they drove by to see the banner, and it was partially hanging down, so they retrieved it.

"The Freeze" newsletter from December 1985 announced the grand opening of the new office at 1556 Jefferson Street. Barbara Stancil wrote about the increase in the mailing list from 1,800 to over 3,000, organizing a bus trip to a San Francisco rally, a walk-a-thon, and a raffle. Their petition drive was successful in delivering over 3,000 Napa County signatures to President Reagan. They also collected more than $1,200 to pay for a full-page advertisement in the *Napa Register*. The week after it came out, Napa's Congressional Representative Doug Bosco signed on as a co-sponsor of a bill to cut off nuclear testing.

The newsletter also announced a spaghetti dinner at the United Methodist Church, $2 for adults and $1 for children, with proceeds to initiate a new year of nuclear freeze activities. It describes four Napa area women who planned to join the Elder's Brigade in Nicaragua to help with the coffee bean harvest. Many Napans participated in the national opposition to the U.S. government's actions against the Nicaraguan government, and 17 people were arrested for occupying the military recruiting center on Jefferson in 1986.

Brad Wagenknecht met Freeze leader Rosemary Gill when he was a high school student. He credits her for going to bat against a local newspaperman who accused him of burning the American flag, telling *Register* reporter Roseann Keegan: "She went up to him and said, 'I've known Brad forever and he may have been a hippie, but he was never disrespectful toward our country.' " Brad and his wife Polly created the *ABC's*, a neighborhood newsletter covering the streets west of Jefferson. For over

20 years, Polly and Brad organized a kazoo band at the Napa Fair parade; she was the band's star bass drummer. They were also members of the food co-op on Main Street below Pearl, where people would trade their labor for bulk discounted natural food. In addition Polly managed the 4-H club, and as her father-in-law John Wagenknecht recalled: "If someone had a dream or concept, she would take off with it."

Inspiring and documenting the activities of the Freeze activists was Al Cardwell, who wrote under the name "Don Quixote de Napa." He produced and distributed the *Napa Free Press*, which he declared the only Democratic paper in Napa. Each issue of the *Napa Free Press* included a dedication to a hero like Napa College teacher Marian Francoz, who "encouraged me to write." Don Quixote described events ranging from Reagan's slashing of funds for social programs (that emptied Napa State Hospital, creating the first homeless population Napans had seen since the Depression), to countless battles by citizens to stop sprawl and over development.

Don Quixote also described the hotly contested plans for the building of the Cinedome Multiplex. Uptown Theater manager Thomas Malloy now says wistfully that he enjoyed the days when independents could run theaters, but there was great pressure to sell to corporations. When city council approved the building of the Cinedome Theater in 1983, it eventually doomed the Uptown.

Across the country, unionized workers felt under attack after Reagan fired 10,000 air traffic controllers in 1980. In Napa, female workers led strikes in both 1981 and 1982. The first was by clerks at Carithers, the last union department store in Napa; the second was an effort brought by housekeepers at Silverado Country Club, the only union hotel in Napa. These strikes created a unique alliance between organized feminism and working-class women, an alliance that enabled Carithers striker Bonnie Lee Barnhill to describe their victory to the union newsletter as "One giant step for womankind!" One local supporter described some of the striking women:

> Loretta wears her dark hair upswept into a bun, is proud of her knowledge of jewelry and her "smart mouth," lives in a trailer with her pigtail daughter, has diabetes. Marlene is a warm rosy woman at midlife. With essential dignity and self-respect, she picketed in her bathing suit, brought iced tea and a beach umbrella to the line.

The Women's Political Caucus collected canned foods for the strikers and organized benefits, including a dance in the Labor Temple on Main Street. Inspired by films of women's historic labor struggles shown at benefits, the youngest striker, at 19, brought her infant to the picket line in a stroller adorned with a sign reading

"Like David Slaying Goliath"

"Don't be a Scab." Linda Dietiker-Yolo, member of the Napa County Commission on the Status of Women, wrote a letter to the manager of Carithers:

> We have been informed that your store's negotiator told union representatives that 'women shouldn't work anyway, I wouldn't let my wife" ... We also hear that most of the clerks are female and that the male clerks have the opportunity to advance, which the women do not have. If the shocking plight of these women is not entirely as represented, perhaps you will inform us. Otherwise, we ask that justice be instituted at Carithers.

The women won the strike and credited the community for its support as they returned to work. Their union newsletter, *Around the Grapevine*, commented:

> It was like David slaying Goliath: a relative handful of determined union women picketed their employer, Carithers, part of a mammoth corporation—in order to maintain a decent living standard and win dignity in their place of work. They never gave up. They walked for four and one half months, from the beginning of spring on through the parching heat of summer—and prevailed.

By 1982 the unionized housekeepers at Silverado Country Club were also on strike. When the employees rejected a contract that reduced pay and benefits, management brought in replacement workers, including members of the Napa-Vallejo Bears, a semi-pro football team now known as the Oakland Raiders. Members of the Women's Political Caucus, Hotel Employees Local 2, and a Teamster's representative joined strikers in blocking traffic. The National Organization for Women sent contributions, and NFL players joined the picket line to show support and voice outrage at the misuse of athletes to break a strike.

Scott Blakey, a *San Francisco Chronicle* reporter, wrote:

> They have been picketing since June 15 in temperatures averaging 90 degrees. 'I think Silverado didn't think we could win: a handful of girls would come crawling back. Well, honey, we ain't crawlin' back to nobody' as Anna Casey states, in a distinct Oklahoma drawl.

Local physician Lanita Witt wrote an open letter to the manager of Silverado, published in the Napa Register:

NAPA

You've lost my business. My mother and aunt from Texas will be visiting me in Napa next week, and my plans had been to treat them to an elegant dinner at the Silverado Country Club. Yet how can I, with pride and a clear conscience, expose my family to an establishment which has restored dignity and jobs to male employees while leaving women in the cold?

We will not have dinner at the Club next week. I will not have dinner at the Club during any subsequent weeks which those women are still debased and treated as unimportant, second-class citizens. I will be ashamed when my mother learns of the conflicts as the Silverado, but proud to let her know that in honor of her years of labor we will not patronize your establishment.

Thirty-five days into the strike the housekeepers and laundry workers accepted a "final offer" of only 29¢ an hour. According to the *Napa Register*, the women cheered heartily at a Fuller Park meeting when their union president Charles Garner stated that they still had the union. Under the new settlement, they would still be earning less than $5 an hour—yet defiant and proud, the women marched back into work together.

In 1986, five years after the end of the clerks' strike, Carithers closed its doors and the women lost their jobs. One by one, factories in Napa were also closing—Rough Rider shut its doors in 1976 and Kaiser Steel in 1983. In February 1986 Napa experienced what the *Napa Register* called "the most disruptive natural disaster to affect Napa County since the 1906 earthquake and the most devastating flood since the winter of 1896." A series of storms saturated the soil, followed by 20 inches of rain in 48 hours. Southerly winds pushed the Napa River to levels none living had seen before. The damage was immense: nearly 5,000 people were evacuated from their homes, 250 homes were destroyed, 2,500 homes were damaged, and three people died. Soscol Avenue turned into a river, ruining hundreds of cars on "Auto Row." Two thirds of Napa's businesses were damaged due to the flood and downtown stores were covered with mud. President Reagan declared Napa a disaster area.

Engineers had warned area residents about the likelihood of a large flood since the 1970s. Downtown was devastated but merchants vowed to rebuild. The *Napa Register* reported that:

Meyers Jewelers president Ian Fuller quipped, "I'll wash all the diamonds and be back in business." Larry Friedman thanked his employees for saving the rest of the store by stacking sandbags until almost midnight; nobody has flood insurance. "If there's such a thing as an 'off the floor sale' we'll have one," Friedman joked.

The Great 1986 Flood brought the town together, creating countless legends of community daring and generosity. No one could have imagined that a decade later, the consequences of the flood management plan would begin to change the face of downtown dramatically.

Chapter Ten

THE RIVER OF CHANGE

The river of change always spills over its banks, inundates the land, and eventually erodes even the most enduring promontories.

—Joseph Amato, *Rethinking Home*

Napa in the 1990s is aptly described by reporter Kevin Courtney as "a kaleidoscope of change, transforming itself into something utterly new." The Flood Control Plan passed in 1998, making possible unprecedented development and gentrification, and the marketing of the city of Napa as both a destination and a lifestyle began. Today, many longtime Napans feel a profound sense of loss, while newcomers herald the upscale shopping and trendy restaurants. Most Napa residents don't recognize the image of luxury and easy living seen by outsiders. As former city councilperson Cindy Watter wrote to the *San Francisco Chronicle*: "It's a real town, with cranky pensioners, blue-collar workers and all sorts of inconvenient people who aren't rich." She explains that Napa is home to the majority of the farmworkers and other underpaid workers in the tourist industry and recalls:

> I was elected to the Napa City Council, and I found myself up to my eyeballs in problems: evaporating sales tax, gang violence, and a working class about to get slammed by the closure of Mare Island. . . . If I had to read one more paragraph about someone cracking open a bottle of cool, crisp Chardonnay as he surveyed his acres from his veranda, I would have to start a class war. Because of my experiences, I can no longer read with composure anything about the romance of the Wine Country.

After the end of the Cold War, the Base Closure Commission targeted California naval institutions. In 1993 the commission shut down six bases in the Bay area alone, including Mare Island Naval Shipyard. Throughout California, major defense companies either abandoned the field or reduced their work forces; historian Richard Rice notes that "conversion became a laborious and painful process and most replacement jobs offered much lower pay levels." Sawyer Tannery, once the hub of manufacturing along the river, closed its doors in 1990.

The River of Change

Like small towns across the country, Napa residents fought and ultimately lost the battle to keep discount chain stores out. In 1996 several "big box" stores were built on wetlands in South Napa, creating an enormous shopping development that threatened the existence of local businesses and department stores. In a few short years, Napa lost Woolworth's, J.C. Penney's, Montgomery Wards, and Merrills Drugstore, sources of both jobs and cherished memories for townspeople. When Woolworth's closed, tears flowed down the face of 72-year-old Myrtle Alric "as dozens of locals expressed their thanks to Alric and the rest of the staff at the lunch counter," Bruce Baird reported that "Black ballons and ribbons marking the death of the downtown institution hung on the booths." Even managers of the Downtown Promotional District and the Napa Valley Conference Bureau dressed in black, while regulars at the luncheonette "pinned the waitresses with black carnations between orders of fries and refills of coffee." Brenda Gee brought her son to remember how her own parents had brought her to the counter 20 years before: "It's just like I remember it—the lights are old and the smells are the same."

In 1998 *Register* reporter Kevin Courtney wrote:

> With a tidal wave of chichi development coming his way and his body showing signs of serious wear and tear, Larry Friedman is closing Brewster's, downtown's most soulful store. "I had planned to stay here forever, this was my life. I knew everybody and everybody knew me. It was a fun place to work." News of Brewster's demise and Larry's medical misfortune had shaken a lot of old-time customers. "I had a woman break into tears. She said, "what am I going to do? I've been coming here as a child." When Larry made an appearance at the store Tuesday, a shopper came up to the busy shopkeeper and whispered, "This is history."

The 1990s were rougher yet for Brewster's. The drought years killed its wet gear business. The opening of Target two years ago was a severe blow to camping gear sales. Over the past five years, "businesses got less and less and less," Larry said. A store that regularly did over $1 million in annual sales found itself doing just two-thirds of that. By October, when no buyer for the store could be found, he and Rachel decided it was time to close shop. The next tenant will sell something a little trendier than tents and foam mattresses, they predict.

Another loss was the death of Ruth Raider von Uhlit . The readers of the *Register* obituaries in July 1995 learned that Ruth had died "surrounded by the tranquility of her much loved urban ranch with hummingbirds hovering outside her bedroom window." John Wagenknecht described her admiringly as "the holdout against giving up farming because she had what she wanted." Kevin Courtney detailed the fight to preserve her home:

> The city's last fruit farm survives in the memories of legions of locals who drove past the sentry eucalyptus trees on Soscol Avenue and up the long driveway to buy the freshest peaches, pears and apples in town. To loyal customers, the ranch and the woman who ran it were beloved vestiges of an earlier, more rural Napa.
>
> A developer, the DeSilva Group, is proposing a major housing project on the 19-acre site: 200 apartments and 83 duplex and triplex units. On Monday night the city's Cultural Heritage Commission debated whether to let the von Uhlit ranch disappear without a physical trace. Historical consultants hired by the developer were unanimous that the ranch property did not meet the usual requirements for historical significance.

Ruth von Uhlit's farm was razed and apartments now crowd out to the street. This was the fate of most orchards, but a few determined farmers continue the prune tradition. Napa Valley College librarian Stephanie Grohs describes one of them:

> Ninety-year-old David Wheatley tasted alcohol once in his youth and didn't like it. He decided early on that he didn't want anything to do with growing grapes, making wine, or "bootlegging." Driving on the private unpaved road to his farmhouse I was struck by the sharp contrast of the landscape. His land on the north side of the road is gently populated with prune and walnut trees in the open fields.
>
> Sitting with Mr. Wheatley in his back garden, surrounded by trees and farm buildings, it is easy to visualize the valley when prune orchards reigned supreme. I could hear the pride in his voice as he talks about his life spent on this bountiful land. By his choice, the view on his side of the dirt road is unchanged.

In 1986, the year of the flood, there were 53,000 people in Napa; by 2003 there were 74,000. Grape production rose to 97.9 percent of the crop value in the county, while livestock and vegetable production declined substantially. The *San Francisco Chronicle*'s Glen Martin described what he found:

The River of Change

Today, the city's economy is keyed to the wine industry. Residents work up valley in the vineyards, wineries and resorts, and locally at restaurants, hotels and wine warehouses. Compared to what was once earned at the steel mills and shipyards, paychecks are paltry.

"There's not much here for our young people now," said Frank Wertz, senior player at Napa Bowl. "They can work in the wineries or at a fast-food place. That's about it. Most of them end up leaving town." While things have begun changing in Napa, residents worry that those changes may not work to their benefit.

Martin contrasted these comments with those of Herb Schmidt, vice president of public affairs for Robert Mondavi Winery, who acknowledged that "not everyone will be happy with the prospect of a Napa that is ritzier and glitzier." But the old Napa—the modestly prosperous blue-collar Napa—is gone forever, he emphasized. The city's best possible future, he feels, lies in a firm partnership with the wine industry. "No doubt about it—there's a downside to the hotels moving in, to increased numbers of visitors," Schmidt said. "But it's inevitable that the town will change. It can't stay the same."

Even local merchants who had embraced the changes in downtown were not immune from its consequences. Sandi Perlman owned Tees and Tops, which supplied customized sports uniforms to local teams. When her landlord tripled her rent, hoping to bring in upscale retailers, she concluded she would have to close her store. "It's a fist in the gut," Perlman told Kevin Courtney, "I sell $25 items. I can't get away from that. That's who I am."

As Napa has been transformed into a service-based economy, jobs in hotels and restaurants, as well as wineries, have become more plentiful. The availability of year-round work, as opposed to the seasonal nature of most agricultural labor, has drawn many new immigrants to Napa. The Latino population in the county rose from about 9,000 in 1980 to over 30,000 in 2004. Writing for the *Los Angeles Times*, Michael Ybarra explained: "These days, the wine business is as much about tourism as it is about agriculture; most Latinos work in the tourist industry." Maria Navarro-Esparza, daughter of Lilia Navarro and co-founder of the Latino Leadership Council, reports that the major challenge faced by immigrant families is paying skyrocketing rents while earning low wages. This tension has resulted in new organizing, tenant activism, and even a housing habitability lawsuit launched by immigrant families.

Immigrant workers are not alone in struggling to make ends meet with the increasing cost of living in Napa. Just as rents for small businesses rose, so did housing costs. Between 2002 and 2004, the median price for houses and condos in Napa County rose from $362,000 to $443,000, a hike greater than in any other Bay Area county. As modest dwellings and trailer parks were razed for the Flood Plan, many longtime Napans were forced to relocate to move affordable communities and some even joined the growing ranks of the homeless.

Just as the people of Napa struggled to preserve the town's rural character, so too did they fight to defend the good jobs that remained. On July 4, 2001, Charles Krug Winery locked out its production workers after they voted unanimously to reject the company's contract offer. *Register* reporter Nathan Crabbe reported that "Almost 50 workers were stopped by winery officials and a security guard as they entered the winery Tuesday for their 6 a.m. shifts, given checks for pay they were owed and turned away." Krug was the only winery with a union production crew, so both sides understood what was at stake. United Food and Commercial Workers Local 186D accused Krug of locking out workers to break the union, which at one time represented over 500 winery workers in Napa County.

The community also understood the importance of the labor dispute, and many people rallied to help the locked-out workers. Maria Navarro-Esparza told Crabbe, "The lockout is a Latino issue but it's also a community issue. We wanted to show our support for their fight." Supporters organized numerous benefits throughout Napa to help the workers pay their bills. At a benefit dinner sponsored by the Unitarian Church in Napa, Carol Wischard, president of the local Communication Workers of America union, presented the workers with a $500 donation on behalf of her members. Crabbe reported that "some workers say they'll send back the checks so that those most in need can receive more assistance."

Napa County and City employees, along with other supporters, contributed to a toy drive for the Krug workers' children, and local activists organized a Christmas party. Aurelio Hurtado, whose wife Rogelia had been locked out after over 30 years with the company, recalled his own efforts to organize the union at Charles Krug in the 1950s. He stood with her on the picket line throughout the eight-month lockout. Also marching with the Krug workers were farm workers from the Hess Collection Winery, who were themselves in the midst of a contract campaign. They had voted to join UFCW over two years earlier, and were still waiting on a first contract. Nevertheless, they were among the most reliable and dedicated supporters of the locked-out workers.

When the Krug workers returned to their jobs in February of 2002, cellar worker Kenny Drost told Nathan Crabbe, "We're going to have to stick together more than we ever did." Many returned to work with pride in having maintained their union, but not everyone was satisfied with the resolution. Aurelio Hurtado's niece and nephew, who had been union shop stewards, were so discouraged by the treatment they received during the lockout that they left the company.

Just months after the lockout ended, new union organizing efforts emerged. The teachers and staff of Napa-Solano Head Start voted to join the SEIU, marking one of the first successful union-organizing drives Napa had seen in years. *Register* reporter Elise Proulx described "screams of victory at the Vallejo Head Start location where the votes were tabulated" and quoted organizer Lorena Melgarejo: "This is just the beginning." Shortly thereafter, county home health care workers also voted to join SEIU. Home health aide Dolores Calderon told Nathan Crabbe, "Everyone thought it was about time." She explained that union representation might mean that for the first time these health-care providers would have access to health insurance benefits for themselves.

In addition to a reinvigorated labor movement, peace activism resurfaced in opposition to the wars in Iraq. According to Kevin Courtney, on January 15, 1991, 500 people met at Veterans Park:

> Offering pleas, petitions and prayers that tragedy be averted. . . . The eleventh hour call for peace in the Persian Gulf featured two hours of anti-war songs and impassioned speeches. . . . America needs thousands of rallies such as this one to convince President Bush to give peaceful options more time to work, organizers said. Speakers lambasted the government's willingness to put American soldiers at risk.

In 2003 the nation was again at war, and activists wondered whether a peace movement would re-emerge. Changes to the town notwithstanding, hundreds of people marched weekly in opposition to the second Iraq War. Some of them, like Rosemary Gill, had protested the Vietnam War; others had been members of the Freeze; some had been infants during the 1991 protests; and yet others did not know there had ever been an anti-war movement in Napa.

As they walked through downtown with their signs and songs, they passed by Napa's past, present, and future. There were the family businesses that have managed to survive on the loyalty of "old Napa" clientele, just blocks away from expensive restaurants bustling with new residents and tourists. There were "Going Out of Business Sale" and "For Lease" signs in storefront windows, evidence of the ongoing transformation. On a daily basis, the local paper describes the latest plans to change the face of downtown Napa. As Kevin Courtney wrote in February of 2004:

NAPA

A vacuum store became a high-end steak house, an Army-Navy outlet morphed into premium offices with a French cafe and a fine art store, a finance company reopened as an upscale wine bar. Yet downtown remains very much a work in progress. Many stores are in an economic slump as landlords, dreaming of big name retailers, raise rents that could force out family-owned businesses. Residents worry that the downtown of the future won't be as welcoming to average-income Napans as the downtown of the past. . . . Is the downtown glass half full or half empty? It all depends on who you are.

Napans disagree about the pace of change. Many reminisce about a time when everyone knew one another and Napa still felt like a small town community, while others dream of moving to towns that resemble the Napa they remember. Controversy over development continues to rage through ballot initiatives and packed hearings at city council meetings.

Development has also threatened historical landmarks. Under the Flood Control plan, the First Street Bridge and China Point Park were set to be demolished. Al Edminster, a volunteer at the Napa Firefighters Museum, led a campaign to save them and found support from Lorraine Dong, of the Chinese Historical Society of California, who wrote to the Napa City Council: "Napa's China Town has special significance for the Society. For many, China Point might appear as just another Chinatown, but it is valuable in providing us with another affirmation of an early Chinese settlement in America's West." Ultimately, Edminster was unable to save the bridge and the trees in China Point Park were cut down in preparation for new bridge construction.

The survival of Napa's family businesses also hangs in the balance. Many residents still like to shop at Family Drug, where customers and clerks recognize each other. They choose to go to Wilsons, the last feed store, reminiscent of an era when many people raised livestock. They frequent Nick Cervone's tailor shop, where Mr. Cervone is at his sewing machine daily. They browse Neff's Office Supplies, once the only place in town to buy stationery. Across the river, The Depot Restaurant continues to be a second home for longtime Napa citizens. Food journalist Elaine Corn writes:

The Depot remains a path to riches incomprehensible to the legions of pedigreed restaurants whose Napa Valley ventures have gone belly-up as malfatti gleefully belly-bombed into the stomachs of contented Depot patrons. The Depot's recipe for malfatti, now made by Clemente Cittoni, was passed down from Teresa Tamburelli in classic show-and-tell style. You won't find this version of malfatti elsewhere in America; it's strictly a Napa thing, also found at the local Ruffino's restaurant and Lawler's Liquors. But the Depot's malfatti came first.

Clemente Cittoni arrived from Italy in 1961 and started out as the restaurant's dishwasher. He learned to make malfatti from Theresa Tamburelli's daughter, Angie Momsen, who crossed the railroad tracks to do the restaurant's books into her 90s; he is now the chef. Cathy Mathews remembers her childhood when "if you got there any later than 6 pm, you couldn't get a table and forget trying to get a stool at the bar. People would be three deep trying to get a drink and a table without having to wait too damn long. You could have shot a cannon in the joint when we were there."

Today a visitor might find a group of postal employees celebrating a birthday in the back room. Waitress Rose Biggs, who has waited tables for over 20 years, flies by with steaming platters of pasta. In the bar Ron Martini holds forth, just like his Aunt Theresa once did. Along the wall is a framed photograph from the 1920s showing workers at Cameron Shirt Company; the pride on their faces sings out, as the past reaches into the present and refuses to let go. At the Depot, as in the town that has transformed around it, the glass is always, at least, half-full.

BIBLIOGRAPHY

Published Material

Amato, Joseph A. *Rethinking Home: The Case for Writing Local History*. Berkeley, CA: University of California Press, 2002.

Baginsky, Yvonne. "Native Napan recalls 'Old days' Fondly." *Napa Register*. 18 November 1995.

Baskin, John. *New Burlington: The Life and Death of an American Village* . New York: W.W. Norton, 1976.

Beard, Yolanda. *The Wappo: A Report*. St. Helena: 1977.

Blakey, Scott. "Sticky Strike at a Country Club." *San Francisco Chronicle*. 15 July 1982.

Barnhill, Bonnie Lee. "Around the Grapevine," *UFCW Newsletter*. August 1981.

Brady-Herndon, Gary. "Paradise." Napa Valley Museum. 2003.

Brennan, Nancy. "A Portrait of Dee T. Davis," *Late Harvest*. Ciao Productions 1984; Mary Ann Doud, Joe Bell and Rita Bordwell, *Napa County Historical Society*, "This Was Napa." Spring, 1998.

Brown, Maddie D. "General Mariano Guadalupe Vallejo and Hubert Howe Bancroft." *California Historical Quarterly*. June 1950.

Bryant, Dorothy. *Confessions of Madam Psyche*. New York: Feminist Press, 1986.

Calkins, Victoria. *The Wappo People*. Santa Rosa, CA: Pileated Press, 1994.

Cerruti, Henry. "Ramblings in California." 1874, MSS C–E 115:2. Bancroft Library. Berkeley, California.

R.G. Collingwood. *The Idea of History*. New York: Oxford University Press, 1996.

Collins, Mildred. "Home is where the Heart is." *Napa Register*. 5 June 2002.

Corn, Elaine. "The Oldest Continuously Operating Restaurant in the Napa Valley," *Napa Valley Appellation*. Autumn 1994.

Couchman, Robert. *The Sunsweet Story*. San Jose, CA: Sunsweet Growers Inc., 1967.

Courtney, Kevin. "Commission wants to preserve von Uhlit home." *Napa Register*. 15 June 2001.

———. "Doctor's orders: Larry must quit," *Napa Register*. 9 December 1998.

———. "Napa Women's Club slowly fading away." *Napa Register*. 15 June 2003.

———. "Pleas, Prayers at Park Rally," *Napa Register*. 15 January 1991.

Bibliography

————. "There Was a War at Home," *Napa Register,* Vintage. April 1980.

————. "Woman saw town, family grow together." *Napa Register.* 6 May 2003.

————. "Mom-and-pop stores losing, moving out of downtown." *Napa Register.* 22 February 2004

————. "Re-inventing Napa." *Napa Register.* 22 February 2004.

————. "Napa Woolworths closing in January." *Napa Register.* 14 October 1993.

Crabbe, Nathan. "Krug Locks Out Production Workers." *Napa Register.* 4 July 2001.

————. "Krug Winery Picketers Upset Nob Hill Managers." *Napa Register,* 5 August 2001.

————. "Napa Health Workers Vote to Unionize." *Napa Register.* 13 December 2002.

Daniel, Cletus E. *Bitter Harvest: A History of California Farmworkers, 1870–1941.* Berkeley, CA: University of California Press, 1982.

Dorgan, Marsha. "Retired teacher recalls Napa's role in World War II." *Napa Register,* Millennium edition. January 2000.

Emparan, Madie Brown. "The Vallejos of California." The Gleeson Library Associates at the University of San Francisco, 1968.

Ernst, Doug. "NFL Players to Picket Silverado." *Napa Register.* 1 July 1982.

Ezettie, Louis. "Looking into Napa's Past and Present." *Napa Register.* 6 August 1977.

Freeze Newsletter. Vol. 3, No. 4. December 1985.

————. "Looking into Napa's Past and Present," *Napa Register.* 28 March 1981.

Gunn, Harry. *History of Napa County.* 1926.

Hanrahan, Virginia. "Historical Napa Valley," Napa County Library. 1998.

Heidenreich, Linda. "Family, Race and Culture in Napa County, California." Barksdale Essays in History, 2000.

————. "History and Forgetfulness in an 'American County.'" Ph.D. Dissertation. UC San Diego, 2000.

Jenson, Peter. *The Great Voice.* 1975.

Johnson, Charles. "Napa's Red Light District." *Napa Register.* 30 March 1963.

Juarez-Rose, Vivian. *The Past is Father of the Present: Spanish California History and Family Legends, 1737–1973, San Francisco and Napa County.* Vallejo, CA: Wheeler Printing, 1974.

Keegan, Roseann. "Rosemary Gill Still Active in National and Local Issues." *Napa Register.* 15 September 2003.

Kimmel, Michael. *Manhood in America, A Cultural History.* New York: The Free Press, 1996.

King, Norton. An Historical Interview, Napa County Superintendent of Schools office. 1967.

King, Phyllis. *Napa Register.* 22 July 1955.

Le Guin, Ursula. *Always Coming Home.* Berkeley, CA: University of California Press, 2001.

Marcus, Gary. "The Dragon's Tail." *Late Harvest,* 1984.

Martin, Glen. "Down in the Valley," *San Francisco Chronicle.* 4 November 2001.

McNally, Sister Mary Gene. "Mariano Guadalupe Vallejois Relations with the Indians of Californians Northern Frontier 1825–1842." Masters thesis, Dominican College of San Rafael. 1976.

Menefee, C.A. *Historical Descriptive Sketch Book of Napa, Sonoma, Lake and Mendocino Counties.* Napa, CA: Reporter Publishing Co., 1873.

Mini, Carolyn and Martin. *Two Families Cavagnaro and Guisto.* Napa, CA: privately published, 1998.

Mumford, Lewis. "The Value of Local History," in Michael Kammen. *In the Past Lane: Historical Reflections on American Culture.* New York: Oxford University Press, 1997.

Napa Daily Journal. 16 March 1901, 14 April 1918, 17 April 1918, October 1918, 14 November 1918, 30 September 1932.

Napa County Historical Society. *Tidings.* March 1987.

Napa County pamphlet. California History collection, California State Library. 1906.

Napanee. 1910, 1911, 1913, 1924, 1925.

Napa Register staff reporter. 27 February 1986.

Palmer, Lyman. *A History of Napa and Lake Counties, California.* San Francisco, CA: Slocum, Brown and Co., 1881.

Parenti, Michael. *History as Mystery.* San Francisco: City Lights Books, 1999.

Penny, Lynn. "Raggedy Ann Meets the Assembly Line." *Napa Register.* 26 May 1972.

Peterson, Marcus Edmond. "The Career of Solano, Chief of the Suisuns." Masters Thesis. Berkeley, CA: University of California, 1957.

Proulx, Elise. "Head Start Goes Union." *Napa Register.* 5 May 2002.

Rice, Bullough and Orsi. *The Elusive Eden.* New York: McGraw Hill, 1996.

Roberts, Brian. "Diversity and the Anglo Forty-Niner." *The Human Tradition in California.* wilmington, DE: Scholarly Resources, Inc., 2002.

Rolle, Andrew. *California History.* Wheeling, CA: Harlon-Davidson, 2003.

Rosenus, Alan. *General Vallejo and the Advent of the Americans.* Berkeley, CA: Heyday Books, 1995.

Sagehorn, Elizabeth. "Over Hill and Valley." *Napa Register.* 7 October 2002.

Sanchez, Rosaura. *Telling Identities: The Californio Testimonios.* Minneapolis: University of Minnesota Press, 1995.

Bibliography

Silver, Mae. *The Sixth Star*. San Francisco: Ord Street Press, 2000.

Smith, Jane. *Napa Register*, 27 June 1994, 8 November 1972. *Vallejo News Chronicle*, 22 March 1972, 28 April 1971, 22 May 1973, 22 May 1974. *Vallejo Times Herald*, 1 May 1977.

Stanley, Anne. "We Had No Choice." *Napa Register*. July 20, 1982.

Starr, Kevin. "Rooted in Barbarous Soil; an Introduction to Gold Rush Society and Culture." *Rooted in Barbarous Soil*. Berkeley, CA: University of California Press, 2000.

Stoll, Steven. *The Fruits of Natural Advantage: Making the Industrial Countryside in California*. Berkely, CA: University of California Press, 1998.

Suberman, Stella. *The Jew Store*. New York: Workman Publishing, 1998.

Swett, Ira L. and Harry C. Aitken, Jr. "The Napa Valley Route." Ira Swett, 1975.

Thomas, Laura. "The Real Historians," *Late Harvest*. Ciao Productions, 1984.

UFCW Newsletter. "Around the Grapevine," Vol. 1, No. 2. Aug.–Sept. 1981.

WPA. Northern California Historic Records Survey. Inventory of the County Archives of California, No. 29. Napa Valley, San Francisco: Government Printing Office, 1941.

Vallejo, Platon. *Memoir of the Vallejos: New Light of the History, Before and After the Gringos Came*. 1914; reprint Fairfield, CA: James D. Stevenson Publisher, 1994.

Verardo, Denzil and Jennie. *Napa Valley*. Northridge, CA: Windsor Publications, 1986.

Watter, Cindy. "Napa is just too real for some people." Letter to *San Francisco Chronicle*, 27 April 2003.

Weber, David J. *The Spanish Frontier in North America*. New Haven, CT: Yale, 1992.

Weber, Lin. *Old Napa Valley: The History to 1900*. St. Helena, CA: Wine Ventures Publishing, 1998.

————. *Roots of the Present, Napa Valley 1900–1950*. St. Helena, CA: Wine Ventures Publishing, 2001.

————. *Under the Vine and the Fig Tree*. St. Helena, CA: Wine Ventures Publishing, 2003.

Wise, Nancy Baker and Christy Wise. *A Mouthful of Rivets: Women at Work in World War II*. san Francisco: Jossey-Bass, 1994.

Ybarra, Michael. *Los Angeles Times*.

Yerger, Rebecca. "Memories of the Combellecks and the Wades." *Napa Register*. 13 October 1996.

————. "Celebrating the sweet life of the candy making Bryant family." *Napa Register*, 13 May 2001.

————. "94-year old remembers days at Washington Street School," *Napa Register*.

————. Interview with Thomas Malloy. *Napa Register.* 23 March 2001.

Yount, George C. *George C. Yount and His Chronicles of the West: Comprising Extracts from the Memoirs and from the Orange Clark Narrative.* Old West Publishing, 1996.

Unpublished Material

Almstrom (Brown), Nancy. Interview by Lauren Coodley, 2003.

Almstrom (Olmstead), Margaret. Interview by Lauren Coodley, 2003.

Amen, Mike. "The Dream Bowl," Unpublished essay. 2003.

Aultman, Chris. Interview by Lauren Coodley, 2003.

Bernard, Bob. Interview by Marie Ross, 1992.

Boyet, George. Interview by Lauren Coodley, 2003.

Brambila, Maria. Unpublished essay, 2004.

Brooks, Pam. Unpublished essay, May, 1981.

Diemer, Joyce. Interview by April Jarboe, 1992.

Dietiker-Yolo, Linda. Letter from Commission on the Status of Women. 26 May 1981.

Dong, Lorraine. Letter from Chinese Historical Society to City Council. 12 June 2003.

Ericcson, Louise. Interview by Shauna Hamernick, 1992. Correspondence with Lauren Coodley, 2003.

Friedman, Larry and Rachel. Interview by Lauren Coodley, 2003.

Grant, Carol Raahauge. Interview by Lauren Coodley, 2000.

Grover, Virginia. Interview by Sabrine Montaldo, 1992.

Guiducci, James. Unpublished essay, 2003.

Hurtado, Aurelio. Interview by Lauren Coodley, 2004.

Joell, Mike. Interview by Lauren Coodley, 2003.

Lamb, Terry. Correspondence with Lauren Coodley, 2003.

Langer, Patty. Interview by Lauren Coodley, 2003.

Malloy, Thomas. Interview by Lauren Coodley, 2003.

Marsh, John. Correspondence with Lauren Coodley, 2003.

Mathews, Cathy. Interview by Lauren Coodley, 2003.

Navarro, Lilia. Interview by Lauren Coodley, 2004.

Northrop, Bob. Interview by Lauren Coodley, 2003.

Northrop, Ruth Bickford. Diary, 1924.

Norton, Virginia. Interview by Lauren Coodley, 2003.

Raymond (Wonder), Dorothy. Correspondence with Lauren Coodley, 2003.

Simms, Ginny. Interview by Marie Ross, 1992.

Stephenson, June. Correspondence with Lauren Coodley, 2003.

Bibliography

Tallman, Virginia. Interview by Lauren Coodley, 2003.

Vintage 2000 Yearbook. Essays by Lois and Jim Engle, 1971.

Von Uhlit, Ruth. Interview by Heidi Wertz, 1981.

Wagenknecht, John. Interview by Lauren Coodley, 2003.

Wallis, Mary. Interview by Carleigh Furlong, 1992.

Weidler, Julian. Interview by Lauren Coodley, 2003.

Wheatley, David. Interview by Stephanie Grohs, 2003.

Wilson, Silvia. Interview by Cathy Mathews, 2003.

Witt, Lanita. Letter to Silverado Country Club, July 16, 1982.

INDEX

Index

The Gilt Edge Bar, located on Main Street in what is now the Wells Fargo Parking lot, was a family bar where workers cashed their checks on Friday nights. This image features Ed Bianchi Sr., who sold the bar to Gene Gattavera; it was destroyed during redevelopment.